WALKING IN
SWITZERLAND

Riffelsee and the Matterhorn, Zermatt ▷

WALKING IN
SWITZERLAND

Brian Spencer

HUNTER
PUBLISHING INC

British Library Cataloguing in Publication
Data

Spencer, Brain, 1931-
    Walking in Switzerland.
    1. Switzerland — Description and travel
    — 1981— Guide-books
    I. Title
    914.94'0473   DQ16

Published by
Moorland Publishing Co Ltd,
8 Station Street,
Ashbourne, Derbyshire,
DE6 1DE England.
Tel: (0335) 44486

ISBN 0 86190 152 5 (paperback)
ISBN 0 86190 153 3 (hardback)

Published in the USA by
Hunter Publishing Inc,
300 Raritan Center Parkway,
CN94, Edison, NJ 08818

ISBN 0 935161 20 1 (paperback)

Printed in the UK by
Butler and Tanner Ltd,
Frome, Somerset.

All illustrations have been
supplied by the Swiss National
Tourist Office.

Contents

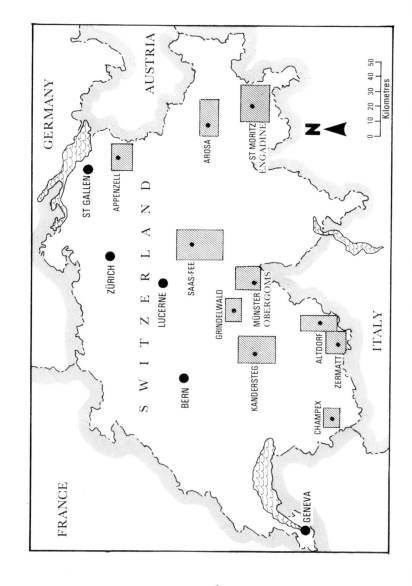

Introduction

Not everyone who visits Switzerland has either the ability or the motivation to climb its highest peaks. So what is it that draws visitors back year after year? The scenery is, of course, the prime reason. Most visitors who are not interested in climbing go to Switzerland in order to enjoy the wonderful scenery at close range; but, like all the best places, the only way really to appreciate the scenery is on foot, and it is with this in mind that this guide has been written.

The guide is a selection of easy to follow walks in ten centres across the country. Some centres are well known, but others are comparatively off the beaten track and probably more attractive as a result. Others are better known in winter than summer, and so gain fresh interest when viewed from a pedestrian angle.

Eight walks are given for each centre, making an ideal ten to fourteen days' holiday when combined with other activities. Although the walks are designed to appeal to families or small groups, some (but only a few) may be longer or harder than usual. Even so, they should be well within the capabilities of anyone used to hill walking in moderately difficult terrain. These walks have been added where a more exciting excursion will help the visitor to appreciate the area more fully.

How to use this guide:

Layout

Each section is devoted to a mountain area or village. The introduction gives a brief description of the place and also indicates a selection of things to do and points of interest nearby. Eight recommended walks in the district are described and range from short walks, often in a valley and ideal for the first day of a holiday, to longer high-level routes suitable for later in the holiday when leg muscles have become accustomed to harder use.

The Walks

A preamble describes the walk in general terms; the route is then described in detail which is intended to be related to the local map

— an essential aid to a walking holiday. The map number of the Swiss Landeskarte survey, or specially prepared local maps, is given at the beginning of each section. In every case these maps have been used for the preparation of the text and spellings used are those found on the maps. Walking instructions are set out so that each part usually refers to readily identifiable features, for instance footpath crossings, woodland, ridge, hut, etc. There will also be an indication of the conditions around the path at that point; rocky, grassy, muddy, uphill or down, etc. Features such as viewpoints, points of interest, special buildings are in italics. Height differences are quoted when they are considerable, downhill as well as uphill.

Directions which indicate left or right relate to those when you face the object mentioned in the text. The only exception is in the case of rivers, when the direction is always determined as though facing downstream.

Distance and Timing
Distance is given in miles and kilometres. The timing is necessarily approximate, and allows for actual steady walking time, but does not allow for stops.

Height Change
In feet and metres, from the start of the walk to the finish, or to some special feature encountered during the walk, eg from the cable car station to the summit. They cannot give all height differences encountered on the walk, but are an invaluable indication of the amount of climbing or descending involved. Heights of mountains and passes are quoted to add local interest.

Grading
Walks are graded into three approximate categories:

Easy   Walking on wide paths with little change of height — suitable in shoes.

Moderate   On well maintained paths. Some height changes, but not exceptional. Boots recommended.

Strenuous   Rocky paths. Some easy scrambling. Steep ascents or descents and much height changing. Fairly long distance. Boots essential.

How to make the most of Alpine Walking

Mountain walking
In Switzerland this does not necessarily mean alpinism. There is a long tradition of footpath building and maintenance, which has given the country an excellent network of high-level pathways throughout the mountain regions.

Paths
Mostly are well signposted and waymarked.

Signposts
Usually give time rather than distance, as this is a far better indication in mountainous regions.

Waymarking
Is usually yellow for low-level paths, and white-red-white at high levels. The colouring may be displayed either as simple painted signs on convenient rocks or trees, or specially-made plates or other similar distinctive marks. In some areas, special colour-coding systems are used, sometimes using numbers, to indicate local walks.

Rights of Way.
It is possible to walk almost anywhere in the Swiss mountains, either by path or across open country, provided you do not walk through private property or over growing crops, including mowing grass. There is usually no objection to anyone walking across a hayfield once the hay has been gathered in.

Nature
Nature accepts man's intrusion in the mountains better than in some of the lower and more crowded regions. Alpine flowers grow in profusion, so fragile that many are specialised in their own local environment. Animals and birds are there to be seen by the observant; chamois will usually be seen as tiny dots crossing some high snow-field well away from danger. Marmots are cheeky creatures, and in some places almost tame. Deer may be accidentally disturbed in forest areas. On high, buzzards and alpine choughs are common while the smaller, seed-eating birds frequent the forest zones. **NB: it is PROHIBITED to pick many of the alpine flowers, and foolish and selfish to pick any.**

Equipment
Should be sufficient for the day. In other words, it should protect

without hindering. Boots should protect the ankle and grip the ground without being unduly heavy. Clothing should be light, windproof and above all protect the wearer from cold weather as well as strong sunshine. It is best to wear lightweight clothing with sleeved and collared shirts to keep the sun off unprotected parts of the body. Carry warm sweaters and a waterproof jacket inside a comfortable rucksack.

Food

This should be no problem in the Swiss Alps. Either carry a picnic or aim to stop at one of the many gasthofs or huts spread conveniently throughout the mountains. Always carry a drink of some kind, and also have some concentrated food tucked away in the rucksack in case of emergency.

Walking in the alps should be an easygoing affair, especially on some of the higher walks; remember, mountain walking should never be a race. Walk at a steady pace; slow down as you get to higher altitudes, because the thinning atmosphere will take its toll of muscles. The paths are safe provided one acts sensibly; never run, especially downhill, on loose rocks or snow-covered ground.

Accommodation

Accommodation is easy to find, and depends on where you are and how much you want to pay. In the valleys it can range from campsites to comfortable farms and guesthouses right through to the high-standard hotels which have made Switzerland famous. Alpine huts are visited on some of the walks; they provide rather basic accommodation, but they are comparatively cheap and the food, though plain, is substantial and always good value.

Travel

The Swiss have developed one of the most efficient transport networks in the world. All forms of transport manage to connect with each other; ferries have trains or buses waiting for them at the tiniest landing stage; and the rail/bus network is the envy of Europe. It is completely integrated, and one can rely on trains and buses arriving (and departing!) exactly as stated on the timetable. Postbuses run through some of the most remote valleys and help to give the mountain walker a car-free holiday. Money-saving tickets are available on the shortest journeys and it helps to check on this beforehand, either at the Swiss Tourist Office in London, at local Information Bureaux, or even on the bus itself.

Cable cars and chair lifts take the drudgery out of most of the steepest ascents mentioned in this guide and are a welcome aid to all except the most ardent purist.

Organised walks

Many holiday areas have a programme of guided walks to suit all tastes and abilities. These are advertised at tourist information offices. Some resorts issue walking badges which are a popular means of recalling a holiday spent in the mountains. A special card is issued by the sponsoring tourist office, stamps are collected by individual walkers at gasthofs and mountain huts throughout the district. Once the requisite number of stamps have been collected, the holder is entitled to a badge. This scheme encourages walkers to reach less known parts of the district.

Mountain Safety

Mountain walking is one of the best forms of exercise, and mountains are places for rest and relaxation, but is is absolutely essential to follow certain rules:

1　Make sure that you and your party are fit to do the walk.
2　Plan your route and check on weather conditions.
3　Be properly equipped for the walk.
4　Always tell someone in advance about your planned route, or leave a note where it can be found.
5　Do not rush. Take your time, especially at high altitudes.
6　Keep to the marked path.
7　Do not dislodge stones.
8　Never be afraid to turn back.
9　Keep calm if something goes wrong. If there is an accident send for help, making sure to specify exactly where it occurred.
10　Keep the mountains tidy and do not pick flowers.

NB: Although information on features, condition of paths etc is correct on going to press, changes may take place. Always check locally concerning current conditions.

Useful Information

Swiss National Tourist Office,
Swiss Centre,
1 New Coventry Street,
London W1V 3HG
Tel: 01 734 1921

Swiss National Tourist Office,
608 5th Avenue,
New York, New York

Provides information on accommodation, maps, rail/bus travel, and is generally helpful on giving advice for holiday planning.

Maps
Available through the Swiss National Tourist Office or McCarta Ltd,

The Map & Guide Shop,
122 Kings Cross Road,
London WC1X 9DS

Edward Stanford Ltd,
12-14 Long Acre,
London WC2

Rand McNally Map Store,
10 E 53rd Street,
New York, New York

The Map Shop,
15 High Street,
Upton-upon-Severn,
Worcs. WR8 0HJ

YHA Adventure Shop,
14 Southampton Street,
London WC2

Insurance
Specialist insurance cover for mountain holidays, can be obtained from:
West Mercia Insurance Services,
High Street,
Wombourne,
Wolverhampton WV5 9DN

NB: mountain rescue in Switzerland can be expensive; it is not always free, as it is in Britain.

Some of the special summer events in and around places covered by this guide

April	Landesgemeinde— open air parliament, Appenzell
May	Corpus Christi procession, Saas-Fee
July	Rose Festival, Weggis (Lucerne)
	William Tell Play, Interlaken
	Jungfrau Ski Race, Grindelwald
	Diablarets Ski Slalom, Engadine
August	Concerts, Engadine
	Confederation Anniversary, Schwyz (Lucerne)
September	Pilgrimage to the Hohen Stiege chapels, Saas-Fee

ALTDORF AND LAKE LUCERNE

Maps

Landeskarte der Schweiz (1:50,000 series). Sheet 5008 – Vier-waldstätter See, and Sheet 246 – Klausenpass (covers the area around the Klausen Pass omitted from Sheet 5008) or Kummerley and Frey. Touristik-Karte (1:50,000) Kanton Uri.

How to get there:

Road:
1   South by motorway to Basel and Zürich, then south by the Gotthard road through Zug and Schwyz to Altdorf.
2   South as above to Basel, then south-east by motorway through Lucerne.
3   Via the Black Forest to Schaffhausen and south through Zürich as 1 above.

Rail:
Mainline trains south from Zürich on the St Gotthard route stop at Altdorf.

Air:
Nearest international airport at Zürich, connection by rail.

The Area

An excellent network of roads, trains, ferries, postbuses and cable cars make Altdorf an ideal base to explore the area east of Lake Lucerne.

The town sits in command of ancient routes along valleys both major and minor. One of these routes is the busy St Gotthard, where the spiralling rail tunnel, built in 1884, is a lasting memorial to the courage of those nineteenth-century engineers, who faced great dangers to build one of the finest railway systems in the world.

Altdorf

To the east is the Klausen Pass, a road often blocked by snow until well into spring. To the north is Lake Lucerne, a lake of many moods, where the ferry system carries the traveller with almost clockwork precision.

The valleys are steep and this can restrict the walking, but conveniently placed cable cars will lift the walker easily to areas of high alpine meadows and easy ridges, where miles of footpaths offer an ever-changing vista of mountains and lakes.

Lovers of alpine flowers, whether expert or just keen observers, will find hours of enjoyment on the high pastures and ridges. From spring onwards, a bewildering spectrum of colour flourishes as soon as the ground is warm enough to encourage growth. Some plants, like the delicate soldanella, are so impatient that they burrow their way through snow or ice, to offer their purple caps to the sun.

The Italian Lake District is not very far away; it is only a couple of hours through the St Gotthard tunnels to Locarno and in the rare event of rain in Altdorf, a trip through the tunnel will often lead to a Mediterranean-like climate. Lucerne is a ferry-boat ride away and it may be on a steam driven paddle-steamer. Lucerne is a busy town of shops, covered bridges and a fascinating garden museum where the story of its glacial past has been uncovered.

William Tell is supposed to have come from Bürglen, a village near Altdorf; the story cannot be proven, but the seat of Swiss democratic freedom is just across the lake on Rütli meadow. The region was the birthplace of the confederation of cantons which we know as Switzerland; in fact the very name of the country is based on the village Schwyz not far way from Altdorf. The walks mentioned in this section can only be a mere handful of those available. As an indication of where to look for the best alternatives, the following areas repay exploration: Muotatal, south-east of Brunnen. A wide high valley with easy access. Mt Rigi, a complex of well-marked footpaths served by funicular railways from Goldau and Vitznau. Klausenpass, east of Altdorf an excellent area for alpine flowers. Engelberg, a mountain resort served by railway from Lucerne.

Useful Information

Local tourist office:
Gotthard –Raststätte
CH 6467, Schattdorf-Uri
Tel: 044 2 5353

Cable Cars, Chair Lifts and Mountain Railways
As well as those mentioned below, there are a number of small, semi-private lifts in the area. Some are literally a box, holding up to four people, and are intended to serve high villages and groups of farms. There will be a notice giving operating times, or a telephone to contact someone in charge. While they may look rather insecure, they are run to strictly controlled standards.

Schattdorf — Haldi (Cable car)
Flüelen — Eggbergen (Cable car)
Vitznau — Rigi (Rack and Pinion railway)
Coldau — Rigi (Rack and Pinion railway)
Alpnach — Pilatus (Rack and Pinion railway)
Kriens/Lucerne — Pilatus (Cable car)
Lucerne — Engelberg (Rack and Pinion railway)
Engelberg — Titlis (Rack and Pinion railway and cable car).

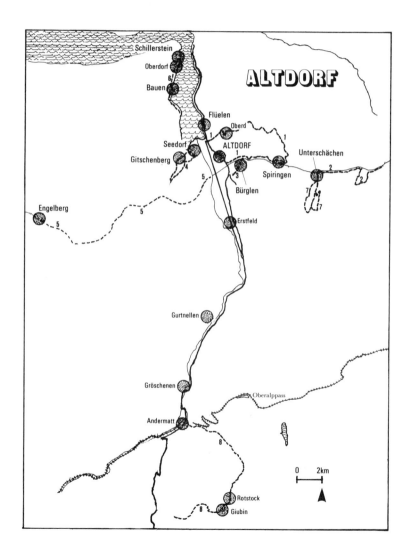

ALTDORF

Schillerstein
Oberdorf
Bauen
Flüelen
Oberd
Seedorf
ALTDORF
Gitschenberg
Unterschächen
Spiringen
Bürglen
Engelberg
Erstfeld
Gurtnellen
Gröschenen
Oberalppass
Andermatt
0   2km
Rotstock
Giubin

16

7 miles (11km), 4 hours. Moderate.
Or
11 miles (18km), 5 hours, if returning to Altdorf by the valley route

---

It always helps to unwind after a long journey across Europe, and this walk is designed with that in mind. A short cable car ride above Flüelen climbs quickly from almost the level of Lake Lucerne to Eggbergen. The path from that point climbs, easily, above the tree line before contouring across the hillside high above the Schächen valley. Small farms take advantage of lush summer grazing on flowery meadows; often the only sound is the melodious clanging of bells around the necks of contented cows, a special breed of alpine cattle which rarely seem camera-shy.

After almost four miles of level path, the signpost down to Spiringen is almost unwelcome, as it marks the end of the high-level walk. Fortunately the path, though steep, is easy to follow into the shade of the valley below. At Spiringen, a decision must be made either to catch the afternoon postbus back to Altdorf or to follow the valley track. Even though the latter necessitates about a mile of road walking, the path is recommended for those with energy to spare. Mostly beneath the pines of the lower valley, it is a shady and interesting stroll, at the end of an exciting introduction to the area.

The Route

□ The bottom station of the Eggbergen lift is just off the main road on the southern outskirts of Flüelen, about $2\frac{1}{4}$ miles (3.6km) from Altdorf town centre. Take the cable car, which rises steeply up the hillside to Eggbergen.

□ A series of tracks lead gently uphill to holiday cottages and hill farms. It does not matter which one is used provided the general direction is to the north-east, and uphill.

The view to the south-west across the southern arm of Lake Lucerne is towards the snowy peaks above the mountain resort of Engelberg. Mount Titlis, at 10,063ft (3,239m), dominates this popular alpine town and it can be visited, together with nearby valleys, on a later walk.

□ The path continues to climb up the side of the wooded spur before crossing a marshy col with a series of tiny lakes. The uphill climbing ends at this point.

Above the col, the view to the north is of the minor peaks around the Hundstock – 7,263ft (2,213m); minor summits by alpine standards, but giants if they could be transported to Northern Europe.

□ Follow a well-defined path around the headwaters of a steep valley which drains south and to your right.

South beyond the Schächen valley the peaks of the Windgällen – 10,459ft (3,187m) rise, with a long serrated ridge running north-east to the Chammliberg – 10,548ft (2,314m) and beyond.

□ Continue along the well-engineered path, around the upper combes of three minor side valleys. Walk ahead over a footpath crossing, and cross the head of the third and final valley.

Pause and admire the view; there is a descent of 2,320ft (707m) beneath, and it could be most tiring for those who are not in training.

□ Turn right, downhill, at a signpost pointing to Spiringen. The path zigzags across high meadows and past attractive timber farmhouses. Lower down the path skirts two small pine woods before entering Spiringen.

Spiringen, small though it may be, has several gasthofs and a shop, making the village an ideal refreshment stop late in the day. Here one can either wait for the afternoon postbus back to Altdorf, or walk home by the valley route.

Optional extension – the Valley Route

The valley path is signposted to Bürglen and starts behind the Post Hotel. It slowly descends on the right of the valley, to the hamlet of Witerschwanden.

□ Go left across the main road and river, then turn right at a track junction. Walk with the river on your right along the forest edge to rejoin the road, then turn left.

□ Follow the road for about one mile (1.6km) until a footpath leads off to the right. Follow it above a small side stream.

□ The path wanders up and down through meadows and pine forest as far as Bürglen. Altdorf is another mile (1.6km) further down the main road.

---

9 miles (14km), 5 hours. Moderate — 3,128ft (953m) descent.

The Klausenpass marks the western boundary between the cantons of Schwyz and Glaurus; it is an ancient boundary, going back to the ninth century, when it marked the division between two different peoples, the Alamans and the Burgundians. Even today this difference can be detected amongst the physical characteristics of people living in valleys separated by high passes such as the Klausen. Both sets of people speak German, or more likely the Schwyz-dütsch dialectic variant, but there the similarity ends. The Burgundians can trace their ancestry back to the Roman Empire, but were driven south-westwards by the Alamans who came from the east in the ninth century.

The best way to do this walk is to leave the car at Unterschächen, at the start of the steep climb to the Klausen, and catch the postbus to the top of the pass. Times of this service are posted at various bus stops and post offices, or can be obtained from the Tourist Office in Altdorf.

From the Klausenpass, the route, after a short initial uphill section, is downhill all the way back to Unterschächen. The walk crosses a steep hillside by a carefully engineered path before dropping down to Äsch and its spectacular waterfall. Plant life on the open hillside consists mostly of the small cushion alpines, which eventually give way to more luxuriant growth in sheltered areas around the tree line.

The Route

□ Catch the postbus from Unterschächen — 3,265ft (995m), to the top of the Klausenpass — 6,393ft (1,948m).

There is an old hotel, the Klausenpasshöhe, marking the summit of the pass. In olden times it was more than a place for refreshment or changing horses; it was a refuge in the desperate conditions brought about by sudden snow storms. Travel was an extremely hazardous undertaking before the technology of snow clearance or sophisticated weather forecasting.

□ Cross the shallow valley opposite the hotel, away from the road. Aim for a group of summer-farms. Turn right behind them and follow a well marked path up the rocky hillside and around the lower bastions of the Chammliberg — 10,548ft (3,214m), which towers high above the path and to your left.

□ Around the corner of the Chammli spur at the end of the climb, the high Stäuben combe is entered. Cross the three mountain streams draining this upper valley. **NB:** in late spring, crossings can be quite hazardous due to melting snow, so care is required.

□ After the final stream, turn right steeply downhill, to cross the main Stäuben river above the tree line.

The rocky slopes of the Chammli spur are covered by tiny cushion alpines such as saxifrages; dwarf gentians bloom in their startling shade of blue and edelweiss hide in small recesses.

□ Still walking downhill, continue round to the right, beneath the cliffs of the Höcheli to a footpath junction.

□ Turn left at the junction and zigzag down the steepest part of the walk as far as the summer-farms at Äsch.

Look back, uphill of Äsch, to its famous waterfall.

□ The path improves as it enters the forest area below Äsch, eventually becoming a jeep track and running parallel to the Vorder Schächen river.

□ Cross the river about a mile above Unterschächen and walk along a walled track past old farmhouses as far as the village.

Unterschächen has a couple of shops, a garage and more important, a welcoming restaurant. A track behind the post office and beneath the church leads to a sheltered grotto which makes an ideal cool shady ending to a hot day.

4½ miles (7m), 3 hours. Easy — 1,434ft (437m), one steep
downhill section.

Here is an easy half day's walk, which can fill an afternoon
following a rainy morning, or half a day devoted to one of the many
excursions possible from Altdorf, perhaps a lake cruise or a
shopping expedition nearby.

The walk follows a pleasant low-level lane from Bürglen to
Schattdorf, where a short cable car ride goes up to the comparatively
level alp around Haldi. To the north-west, the southern arm of
Lake Lucerne, the Urner See, shines invitingly. Beyond Haldi a
steep downhill path leads into the Riedertal valley and an easy
forest path back to Bürglen.

The Route

□ From the centre of Bürglen, by the William Tell museum, follow
the signposted track through meadowland to Schattdorf.

□ The Haldi cable car is on the north side of the village and will be
more or less the first thing encountered on reaching Schattdorf. Use
the cable way to reach the farm alp of Haldi.

□ Follow the track to the right, away from the upper station, past a
series of small farms and summer holiday homes.

*The view to the north is of the Urner See cradled between the arms of
the hills above Flüelen on the right and Oberbauen opposite. Further
round on the left, the peaks above Engelberg rise up above the Reuss
valley, the route to the St Gotthard Pass, one of the major passes south
from Switzerland.*

□ Keep on the path away from the cable car. Use this path to climb
above Haldi, then out on to a grassy ridge to the north-east of the
settlement.

□ At a signposted junction of paths, turn left, at first along the ridge
and then right, down the steep valley side by a zigzag path into the
Riedertal forest.

*In early summer before haymaking, the meadows are a riot of
flowers; the narcissus-flowered anemone is especially plentiful
around here, together with its sister the bright sulphur-yellow
anemone.*

□ Walk down the valley, alongside its stream, as far as a wayside shrine where the track divides.

□ Turn left at the shrine, continuing to walk downstream, mainly beneath mature pines.

□ The path leaves the confines of the forest at its boundary with farmland and also moves away from the stream.

□ Gradually swing round to the left on an improving path through meadows and past small farms until you regain the centre of Bürglen.

Switzerland's legendary hero, William Tell, is supposed to have been born in Bürglen and the site of his stand against the tyrant Geissler is nearby. There is a Tell Museum in Bürglen housing a collection of chronicles, documents and other mementoes relating to this heroic period of Swiss history, when a series of tiny cantons amalgamated into a single democratic nation.

Lake Lucerne

6$\frac{1}{2}$ miles (10$\frac{1}{2}$km), 3-4 hours. Moderate.

On the west side of the Reuss Valley and dominating Altdorf, a long ridge rears up into the sky, its first peak, the Gitschen — 8,336ft (2,540m) — appears to be almost vertical when viewed across the lower valley. But the Gitschen is only one of a series of 8,000ft-plus peaks which make the impossibly steep wall above the Gitschital Valley.

This walk, after the initial use of the Gitschenberg cable lift from Seedorf, climbs high beneath craggy peaks into the upper reaches of the Gitschital. It then returns to the main valley by a forest path, alongside the Palanggen stream flowing out from the Gitschital. This is an exciting route in close proximity to high mountain peaks, and it is easy to follow without strenuous effort.

To reach Seedorf, do not use the N2 Autobahn, but take instead the minor cross-valley road from Altdorf.

The Route

□ Take the cable car from Seedorf to Gitschenberg.

□ Walk away from the upper station on the path which contours easily through the upper half of the Gitschital valley. Cross high alpine pasture to the old farmsteads at Hohenegg.

□ The path now descends gradually through dense forest, broken only by avalanche scars, as far as the high-level summer settlement at Gitschitaler Boden.

Spend a little time exploring the area around Boden; the wooden buildings are built on ancient foundations. People have brought their animals here almost since man first settled in the area, not long after the end of the last ice age.

The walls of the Gitschen ridge tower directly above Boden and culminate in the Brunnistock, at 9,688ft (2,952m), and the Blackenstock, at 9,616ft (2,930m); both seem to blot out the sky to the north. Lower and more broken ridges made the south wall of the valley an interesting place to explore, especially if you are interested in alpine flowers.

□ Turn left away from the farm buildings of Boden and walk down the valley. The path skirts the top of a steep cliff before entering the forested valley slopes as far as Rüti.

There is a cable car down from Rüti which could be used to shorten the walk if necessary. This will take you into the main valley a mere ³/₄ mile (1.2km) from Seedorf.

□ If walking all the way, use a zigzag track which makes its way from the upper station of Rüti; first away and then back under the cable, and with one final loop beneath it once again, it enters Oberdorf by a narrow road. Refreshments are available in the nearby village of Seedorf.

The road leads back across the valley to Altdorf, but to collect a car at Seedorf there is a ½ mile (1.2km) walk along a quiet lane to the north-west of Oberdorf.

William Tell monument in Altdorf

Using the Brüsti cable car from Attinghausen — 15 miles
(22.5km), 7 hours. Strenuous.

Uphill
Brüsti to the Surenenpass — 2,514ft (766m) in 3¼ miles (5km).

Downhill
Surenen to Engelberg — 4,171ft (1,271m) in 11¾ miles (19km).

This is a hard walk, but one which if undertaken in the right frame of
mind and state of fitness, should make an expedition which will be
remembered for many, many years to come. Even with the help of
the Brüsti lift from Attinghausen, to take all the hard work out of
the steep initial climb, the track above Waldnacht along the Grat
ridge is still hard work, especially on a hot day. On such a day it
helps to learn from the locals and follow their example by making
the earliest possible start to the climb.

From the summit of the Surenen Pass, the way is all downhill
except for one or two annoyingly steep little diversions around
knolls or other obstacles. At first the path descends into the wild
bowl of Seewen, dotted with inviting cool shallow pools. Seewen is
a good place to hunt for rare alpine flowers or watch the dainty
chamois, or even the majestic ibex, pick their way across seemingly
impossible rocky crags. Lower down, the first alpine farms are met;
at these, there is a welcome chance to buy simple food and drink.
Eventually the mountain valley widens and with it the home
pastures of Engelberg are reached. The massive towers of the abbey
church beckon the walker along the final stages of the walk into the
village, and after a welcome refreshment break, there is a train back
towards Lake Lucerne. Use either the ferry to reach Flüelen or the
bus from Stans to return to Altdorf.

The Route

☐ Use the cable car from Attinghausen to reach Brüsti.

☐ Walk through the scattered mountain settlement and take the left
fork about 100yd (91m) above the top station. The path along this
first section is through low-growing scrubby pine trees.

☐ Start to climb the Grat ridge which is in front and to the east of the gap which denotes the Surenen Pass.

□ Join the path which has climbed on the left, from the Waldnacht valley.

□ The final stage to the summit of the pass is steep and could still hold patches of snow. Take great care and do not rush things.

Pause on the pass and admire the view. Peak after peak rises up on either hand. Directly ahead, above the Surenen valley is Mount Titlis, first climbed in 1744 by four peasants from Engelberg.

□ Start to walk downhill into the Seewen basin and its five tiny lakes.

The basin is a typical combe formed by glacial action and is an ideal place to find rare alpine flowers. Photograph them by all means, but on no account should they be picked. Not only does this kill the plants, but it is a serious offence in Switzerland to take rare alpine flowers.

□ The path follows the main valley in a series of descending steps as far as a tiny wayside shrine on the Blacken alp.

□ After crossing a little over a mile of fairly gentle terrain the path divides. Take the right fork, steeply into the ravine of the final high level section of the valley.

□ As the angle eases, summer farmsteads at Stäfeli are reached and then Alpenrösli where there is a simple, but very welcome restaurant.

□ Join a steadily improving road which is followed through meadowland all the way down to Engelberg.

A dramatic waterfall can be seen to the right of the track near Herrenrüti.

Engelberg, a popular tourist village with a cable car system for Mount Titlis, is connected by a rack and pinion railway to towns surrounding Lake Lucerne. The monastery, which was founded in the twelfth century, owned the whole valley until it was invaded by the French in 1798. Its abbey church is especially interesting and is decorated in the sumptuous style of the eighteenth century Baroque School. The organ is one of the largest in Switzerland and special concerts are given from time to time.

9½ miles (15km), 4 hours. Easy.

If you have been following the walks of this section of the book in their chronological order, then this walk offers a pleasant rest day to follow the Brüsti to Engelberg high-level route. The walk should also appeal to car drivers as it entails the very minimum of driving.

With the typical efficiency of the Swiss, ferry services on Lake Lucerne run like clockwork, and regular services call at the smallest resort along the shoreline.

The walk follows the shore between Isleten and Bauen before climbing quite steeply to Seelisberg where a diversion leads down to Rütli's idyllic lakeside field. This is the cradle of the Swiss Confederation, where the country's hard-won liberty is still celebrated in traditional manner, with males of voting age entitled to air opinions on matters of great importance both national as well as local.

The route continues above the Schillerstein rock, to Treib and its quaintly decorated inn where a convenient ferry returns to Flüelen.

The Route

□ Take the ferry from Flüelen to Isleten. Follow the quiet lakeside road as far as Bauen.

Attractive restaurants and gasthofs offer tempting refreshments along the way.

□ Climb out of Bauen by a narrow track which starts beyond the last houses in the village. The path visits numerous small farms as it wends its way through steep meadows, offering constantly changing views of the lake far below.

□ Ignore any side paths until you meet a road.

□ Turn right along the road and walk into Oberdorf village, which should make a good stopping place for lunch. There are shops and gasthofs as well as a small park with convenient benches.

□ About 200yd (183m) along the road, a signposted path on the right leads steeply down to the Rütli meadow by the lake shore.

Plaques tell the story of this shrine to democracy.

□ Climb back uphill through mixed woodland.

□ At a footpath junction, turn right along the contouring path which follows an easy route above the crag of Schillerstein.

□ The path reaches the steep zigzag road to Treib. After a few yards turn right away from the road and walk down a clearly marked path through woodland and meadows to the lake.

The heavily decorated half-timbered gasthof will make the wait for the ferry a pleasant end to an enjoyable walk.

One of Switzerland's well-marked hiking trails

8 miles (13km), 4-5 hours. Strenuous.

The Brunnital and Unterschächen valleys seem to be shut in by mountains which rise almost vertically from their depths. Halfway up the sides of the Brunnital, a comparatively level area, created by some long-vanished glacier, is dotted with small farms where the local people take their cattle and goats for the summer grazing. Using the lush pasture created by almost unlimited sunshine on soil well dampened by melting snow, friendly farmers spend the summer months converting milk into butter and cheese. Unlike some remote areas, the people on this alp welcome visitors, and even if you have no mutual spoken language, signs and smiles will quickly evoke a response from the shyest bystander.

After making contact, a glass of deliciously cool milk may be offered, or perhaps an invitation to rest in a simple, but immaculately clean, living room.

At the end of the walk, in order to avoid a steep and rocky descent, it is possible to use a private lift from Vorder Boden. This is only a glorified box, but it is quite safe; the only problem may be in finding someone to operate the machinery! Perserverance is necessary, but the reward will be an easy descent to the valley bottom.

The Route

□ From Unterschächen, walk south along the side road away from the village and into the Brunnital valley.

□ Where the valley track begins to climb away from the river, turn left on a side path across the river.

□ Follow the well-defined path uphill through sparse pine forest on rocky ground.

□Climb uphill and work your way following the path along the crag which looms above, and at first seems impossible to climb.

□ The climbing is easier once the crag has been surmounted. Turn right on top and pass a series of farm settlements, crossing four small streams along the way.

□ Beyond the fourth stream, turn right downhill through forest, to the main valley stream.

□ Cross over to the far side of the valley and climb up to a junction of paths.

□ Turn left on the valley track, which climbs at first steeply, then more gently uphill to the farms of Brunni.

The rocky wall which closes the valley to the south is the ridge between the Ruchen massif – 9,452ft (2,880m), and the Windgällen – 10,460ft (3,187m). Chamois can often be seen on grassy ledges between snowfields on their lower slopes.

□Climb steeply to Sittlisalp, the highest group of farms in the Brunnital area.

□ Keep to the right of the farms and follow a gentle path across the high pasture as far as the Vorder Boden farmsteads.

□ Look out for the upper cable station and also someone to operate the lift.

□ Descend either by the cable car, or otherwise follow the steep path down into the lower reaches of the Brunnital.

□ Follow the wide track back to Unterschächen and welcome refreshments.

14 miles (22.8km), 6-7 hours. Strenuous — 2,248ft (865m) ascent.

The St Gotthard Pass, one of Europe's highest road passes, marks another boundary between two major ethnic groups. To the north, the people are German-speaking, but once over the pass the change is abrupt, the language is Italian and the people are shorter, darker, and quite definitely Mediterranean in origin.

This walk starts from the St Gotthard Hospice, using the old road to get there. Now that a road tunnel has cut through the mountain range, the old road has reverted to the romantic, adventurous route it was before the advent of heavy traffic. A journey by road over the pass is to move back at least thirty years in motoring experience.

The railway has for many decades run through a tunnel beneath the St Gotthard in a series of loops and turns, and is one of the major all-weather routes between north and south Europe. No main-line expresses call at Andermatt, hidden away in its tiny no-man's land at the head of the Reuss Gorge, but it is at the junction of the two major alpine railways linking the Rhône and Rhine. The town is on a branch line from Göschenen on the main north/south route.

To reach the start of the walk it will be necessary, if using public transport, to travel by an early local train to Andermatt and then catch the postbus over the pass to reach the hospice. The walk returns to Andermatt so book a return on the train. If travelling by car, leave it in Andermatt and catch the postbus to the summit of the St Gotthard. Check the timetable before starting.

The Route

□ Travel by road from Andermatt to the St Gotthard Hospice.

St Gotthard Pass – 6,919ft (2,108m) is in a sombre setting of dark lakes surrounded by glacier-worn rocks. Rocky peaks tower all around to give the place a 'shut in' feeling. The hospice, built to help travellers in this wild inhospitable place, is on the site of a chapel founded about 1300 in honour of the German Saint Gotthard, Bishop of Hildesheim (near Hanover).

□ Turn left away from the road to follow the reservoir access track up to Lago della Sella. (Notice how the names have changed from Schwyzer-dütsch to Italian).

□ Walk along the shoreline and cross the main feeder stream at the far end of the reservoir.

□ Climb, by a series of zigzags, to a group of ancient farm buildings on a sunny alp at point 2522.

□ Follow the track, which winds steadily around the rim of the upper combe. The path then makes its way between a series of crags to the summit of the Sella pass — 9,111ft (3,002m).

□ Walk down the scree-covered slope to the Unteralp Pass, and then cross glacier-worn rocky slabs into the upper valley of Unteralp.

□ Follow the white-red-white waymarks down a sharp-nosed rocky ridge, to the first of the high alpine grazing areas at the confluence with the Bortwasser valley.

□ Call in at the Vermigel alpine climbing club hut for refreshments.

□ The angle of descent becomes easier once the path enters the lower valley below the hut.

□ Walk past a series of summer farms along their access road.

□ Keep to the right hand bank of the river all the way down into the valley.

□ Enter Andermatt by turning left away from the railway line.

Andermatt, before the coming of the rail and road tunnels, was an important staging post on the St Gotthard road. Travellers were often forced to wait here for days or even weeks, when the pass was blocked with snow. Today its importance lies in the fact that it is at the junction of mountain railways crossing high passes. From the east, the 'Alpine Express' from Brig crosses the Furka Pass to drop down to Andermatt, before climbing out over the Oberalp pass on its way via Disentis to Chur, in the Rhine valley, and on to St Moritz by the Rhaetian line.

GRINDELWALD

Maps

Landeskarte der Schweiz (1:50,000 Series) Sheet 5004 — Berner Oberland

How to get there:

Road:
1   Via Basel and Bern by motorway, then south and east through Thun to Interlaken. Grindelwald is to the south-east along a minor road.
2   From Basel, either via Zürich or more directly to Lucerne then south-west via Interlaken.

Rail:
Main line by international express to Interlaken. Change to the mountain railway at Interlaken Ost (East) station for direct trains to Grindelwald.

Air:
International airports at Zürich and Bern, then rail via Interlaken.

The Area

There is probably nowhere in Switzerland which has such a dramatic setting as Grindelwald. Gigantic mountains rear up over 13,000ft (3,962m), with sheer north faces rising directly from the meadows of this little town. So steep are these faces that they can only hold summer snow on a few narrow ledges. This is the land of the awesome Eiger, scene of many mountain tragedies; the silent Mönch, aptly named from its likeness to a monk's cowl; over all towers the serene pure white summit of the Jungfrau. Glaciers flow

The Schilthorn cable car

in frozen disarray between the peaks, their icy crevasses waiting to trap unwary climbers.

Grindelwald sits on a high, sun-trapping plateau; to the south is the giant wall of the Jungfrau massif, but the hills on its north and west sides are much gentler. Between these hills and the central plateau are miles of spectacular and yet easy walking. The use of one of the most famous mountain railways in the world, or the many cableways in the area, helps the walker to reach breathtaking viewpoints and also provides many downhill walks on easily graded paths, part of the excellent system of mountain tracks around the valley sides.

A trip on the Jungfrau railway, while expensive, is a must for anyone staying in the area. This famous rack-and-pinion railway takes the traveller above the Kleine Scheidegg mountain resort, then through the heart of the Eiger to a viewing station, the Eigerwand, on the steepest section of the mountain. From here the line spirals inside the mountain, appearing briefly on the Eismeer above the Eiger glacier, and then finally arrives at Europe's highest railway station on the Jungfraujoch pass.

Another long but worthwhile journey up a mountain is the cable car ride up the Schilthorn, probably better known as Piz Gloria since it featured as such in the James Bond film *On Her Majesty's Secret Service.* The Schilthorn lift starts at Stechelburg above Lauterbrunnen, then climbs to Gimmelwald and Mürren by the longest cableway in the alps, all the way to the summit.

There is a great deal for the walker to enjoy around Grindelwald, and anyone with the least interest in mountains and mountain walking cannot help being thrilled by the experience of exploring its many highways and byways. The walks mentioned in this section can only be a selection of the many offered. As an indication of potential, the areas chosen give ample scope for further exploration and all are accessible, either by mountain railways, chairlifts or cable cars; the First chairlift, south-east from Grindelwald, links easy walks on the Faulhorn even as far as Schynige Platte. To the west is Kleine Sheidegg and beyond the Tschuggen mountain are the resorts of Wengen and Lauterbrunnen. Further afield, on a high alp, is Mürren, reached either by rail from Lauterbrunnen or the Schilthorn cable car. Many lower level walks can be found around Interlaken or by the shores of its twin lakes.

Useful Information

Tourist Office
Verkehrsbüro Grindelwald
CH-3818 Grindelwald
Tel: 036 53 12 12

Glacier Viewing
Eiger glacier — from Kleine Scheidegg, or Eismeer on the Jungfrau railway.
Glessen glacier — across the valley from Mürren or the Schilthorn.

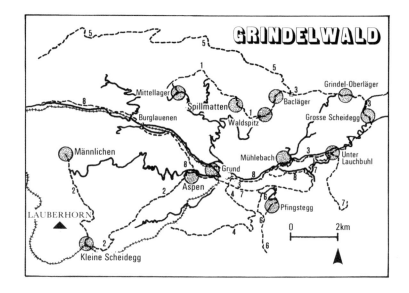

Accommodation
From first class hotels to well-appointed campsites.
Holiday apartments available.

Mountain Railways
Bernese Oberland: Interlaken (Ost) — Lauterbrunnen — Grindelwald.
Schynige Platte: Wilderwill — Schynige Platte
Lauterbrunnen — Mürren — Allmenbuhel
Wengenalp — Lauterbrunnen — Kleine Scheidegg
Jungfrau: Kleine Scheidegg — Jungfraujoch
Interlaken — Harder

Cable cars, Chair lifts
From Grindelwald — Pfingstegg (cable car)
                   First (chair lift)
                   Stat Männlichen (gondola)
From Kleine Scheidegg — Lauterhorn (chair lift)
From Wengen — Stat Männlichen (cable car)
From Stechelburg — Mürren-Schilthorn (cable car)

WALDSPITZ AND BUSSALP FROM THE FIRST CHAIR LIFT

---

5 miles (8km), 3-4 hours. Moderate.

First, the name of this three-stage chair lift from Grindelwald, has nothing to do with its order in the number of lifts in the area; the word *first* simply means a ridge. The title is therefore descriptive of the siting of the upper station. Here ridges and peaks can be seen in all directions, and the cableway is an easy way to climb the 3,650ft (1,112m) required to enjoy them to the full. The first-ever passenger-carrying cable car, the Wetterhorn, was opened on 27 July 1908; it carried sixteen passengers at a time to a viewing station above the Oberen Grindelwald glacier.

Anyone visiting Grindelwald for the first time cannot fail to be impressed by the sight of the awesome spectacle of the Eiger — 13,030ft (3,970m) high, towering, in an almost sheer wall of rock and ice, 9,583ft (2,920m) above the village. To appreciate fully the majesty of this mountain scenery, it is necessary to get as high as possible on the opposite side of the valley; this walk is ideal for that purpose. Not only does it gain height easily, but the paths followed are mostly across open hillsides where the ever-changing views can be appreciated, making the walk an overture to a holiday in the Grindelwald area.

The Route

□ Use the three stages of the First chair lift from Grindelwald to reach the top station. (The Firstbahn — lower station — is off the main street about half-way between the Information Bureau and the village church).

The highlight of this walk is the view across the valley. It becomes apparent almost as soon as you leave the chairlift. All the peaks are seen in their eternal splendour. From left to right the view ranges in one solid wall of rock, snow and ice, with complex side ridges reaching down towards Grindelwald. The Wetterhorn soars above Grosse Scheidegg at the head of the valley; next comes the jagged crest of the Schreckhorn which seems almost to cower beside the Eiger, that infamous peak whose north wall has been the scene of so many fatal climbing accidents. The shoulders, but not the summit of the Mönch can be seen, separating the Jungfrau from the rest of the giants. Summits only slightly less in height march away to the south-west and complete this panorama of alpine grandeur.

□ Walk uphill away from the chair lift towards a footpath junction.

□ Make two left turns and follow the white-red-white waymarked zigzag path, steeply downhill through a line of crags.

Take care on the rocky and sometimes slippery path through the crags.

□ Cross a broad combe along the upper edges of a steep crag, then go downhill on alpine pasture to the group of summer farms called Bachläger.

□ Cross the Mühlebach stream, beyond which the path follows a more level route as far as the Waldspitz mountain hotel.

The Waldspitz is situated above the upper limits of the tree line; the trees make an ideal foreground to frame photographs of the peaks on the opposite side of the valley.

□ Climb slightly uphill away from the hotel, skirting a pine wood. Follow the well-made path on a level, contouring route, around a broad grassy spur.

□ Work your way, by path, across a rocky pine covered slope to Spillmatten.

□ Turn right, climbing steadily, between the barns and little farmhouses of this suntrap.

□ Turn left on a path signposted to Bussalp and climb across the scree-covered lower slopes of the Rötihorn then over the Boneren stream.

□ Join a rough road at Oberläger and follow it to the left, downhill, to Bussalp. Buses run from here back to Grindelwald.

9½ miles (15.3km), 4-5 hours. Easy/moderate — 4,296ft
(1,309m) descent.

The group of summer farms and restaurants around the high-level
Kleine Scheidegg station is an important staging post on the rack
and pinion railway. It climbs in a cleverly designed corkscrew
through the Eiger, and its neighbour the Mönch, to reach its airy
upper station on the Jungfraujoch at 11,336ft (3,454m). Kleine
Scheidegg is at the junction of the lines which climb from
Grindelwald and Lauterbrunnen. On this walk the station marks
the end of the high-level section of the route, height which has been
easily reached by using the Männlichen gondola lift.

A short climb from the upper station soon reaches the summit of
Männlichen. Next, an easy-to-follow, well-made path works its
way across the eastern slopes of the Lauberahorn, offering ever-
changing views of the north face of the Eiger. Kleine Scheidegg
makes a comfortable lunch stop before the downhill path is
followed all the way back to Grindelwald.

The Route

□ The Männlichen lift starts from the lower part of Grindelwald
village, close to the Grund station of the Jungfraujoch railway. Use
the gondola lift to reach the world-famous hotel and its restaurant,
on the upper slopes of Männlichen mountain.

□ Turn right away from the top station and follow the rocky
signposted path, with white-red-white waymarkings, to the summit
of Männlichen — 7,690ft (2,343m).

*The vantage point of Männlichen's summit offers a unique
panorama of the Lütschine valley and of the villages around
Grindelwald in the Upper Schwarze (black) Lüschine valley, as well
as glorious views of the Wetterhorn massif and the Eiger. The
Männlichen ridge is a popular take-off point for hang glider pilots.*

□ Retrace your steps past the restaurant and gondola lift and walk
as far as the top of the Teufenschluecht skilift (Teufenschluecht
means Devils Ravine). Follow the wide, reasonably level path
around the rocky shoulder of Tschuggen.

□ Cross a small stream and bear left at a footpath junction. Walk gently downhill over alpine pasture beneath the Lauberhorn summit to the Grindelwaldblick restaurant. (Viewpoint).

The slopes of the Lauberhorn will be better known in winter to followers of downhill ski competitions. This area has some runs of a very high standard, and is used by all the top skiers.

□ Climb uphill, a little way, to the Kleine Scheidegg railway station.

Perched on its high col beneath the Jungfrau and the Eiger, Kleine Scheidegg station is a busy junction full of walkers, climbers, and other travellers to and from the Jungfraujoch. An interesting half hour or so might be spent watching the efficient running of this unique railway.

The Schilthorn ('Piz Gloria') – 14,288ft (2,960m) is to the east across the Lauterbrunnen valley; it is reached by a double stage cable car via Stechelberg from Mürren.

□Walk downhill towards Grindelwald, following the railway track for a short distance and then bearing left towards the bottom of the Arvengarten chair lift.

□ Turn left below the chair lift. Then go down to, and cross, a small stream. Climb to the group of farm buildings at Bustiglen.

□Turn right on reaching Bustiglen to follow the broad grassy shoulder above the stream. Leave the pasture and enter the pine forest of Itramenwald.

□ Walk downhill through the forest for about 2 miles (3.2km) as far as an access road at Bocketor.

□ Where the road swings left across the grassy shoulder of the upper meadow, turn right and cross a shallow valley, passing several wooden barns on the way.

□ Reach the metalled road and turn right to reach the Aspen restaurant.

□ Follow the narrow lane behind the Aspen as far as the valley road. Turn right towards the river. Cross the bridge and walk into the Grund area of Grindelwald.

3½ miles (5.6km), 2 hours. Easy (bus from Grindelwald to Grosse Scheidegg).

Or

10 miles (16km), 4-5 hours. Moderate (walking all the way from Grindelwald — 2,970ft (905m) climb).

This is a walk which can be adapted to suit the day or the inclinations of the party. To walk all the way from Grindelwald to Grosse Scheidegg is a stiff pull, but the climb has its rewards. The old track used on this walk climbs from Grindelwald through fields planted with fruit trees and maples, and dotted with attractive timber buildings. In spring and early summer the meadows are a kaleidescope of colour when the flowers are at their best, but autumn brings out the beauty of the maple leaves once they have been touched by early frosts.

From Grosse Scheidegg, the way is easy and almost level along a carefully graded track. Buses run from Grindelwald to Grosse Scheidegg and so the second and higher part of the walk can easily be followed on one of those days which start infuriatingly wet, only to improve after lunch. The day will therefore be far from wasted if you take advantage of the bus to gain the 2,970ft (905m) from Grindelwald.

The walk has some of the best views of the Wetterhorn, whose dark cliffs seem to rise directly above the col of Grosse Scheidegg.

The Route

If you decide to use the bus, then join the walk by following the last four instructions below.

□ If you intend walking all the way from Grindelwald, walk out of the village along the Grosse Scheidegg road, following yellow waymark signs to the top of the first hairpin bend above the junction with Terrasenweg.

□ Turn left on the minor road to Mühlebach. Cross a small river and climb the intervening ridge before going down to the Horbach river.

□ Turn right at the road junction, cross the Horbach and follow the lane around the broad, meadow-covered spur, into the Bergelbach valley.

□ Cross the tree-shrouded Bergelbach river and climb out through open meadowland to a junction of five lanes.

□ Walk ahead, steadily uphill, following the north side of the Brüggbach valley to join the Grosse Scheidegg road at Unter Lauchbühl.

□ A group of farm buildings mark the start of the steepest section of the private road which zigzags uphill to Grosse Scheidegg. Leave the road above the second hairpin where it touches the Brüggbach stream.

□ Follow the path, which stays close to the stream, crossing the road about eight times all the way to Grosse Scheidegg.

The footpath which climbs out of the Grindelwald basin traverses narrow belts of forest, open meadows and follows a mountain stream to reach the alpine zone around the col. There is an excellent restaurant at Grosse Scheidegg which is renowned for its views of the north face of the Wetterhorn, Weisshorn and of course the Eiger.

□ Turn left and follow the track northwards along a broad ridge beyond the hotel.

□ Left at the junction of tracks beneath Gemsberg, 8,727ft (2,659m) and cross a series of streams flowing through the broad Heidbühl combe. Walk up to the group of alpine farms at Grindel-Oberläger.

□ Following signposts to First, ignore a track on the left, walk across broad Alp-Grindel between the lower and upper stations, respectively, of two ski lifts serving the winter snows of this sunny hollow.

□ The upper station of the First lift marks the finish of this walk, but there is a path down to Grindelwald for those with energy to spare. It follows the steep spur south to join a narrow track close by Egg station. This track can be followed as far as the junction beyond the Bort restaurant where a left turn leads to Mühlbach and Grindelwald

5$\frac{1}{2}$ miles (9km). 4 hours. Moderate/strenuous.

The Eigerwand, the north wall of the mountain which has claimed so many lives in the past, rises apparently vertically above the wooded slopes of the Rinderalp. A path from Alpiglen, the second halt on the Grindelwald to Kleine Scheidegg section of the Jungfraujoch railway, climbs through the upper limits of the pine forest beneath the Eigerwand. The mountain wall towers threateningly above the path, with glaciers and permanent snowfields clinging to an impossibly steep face.

On the second stage of the walk, there is a complete change of scene, because on rounding the Boneren crags which mark the lower limits of the Hörnli ridge running north-east from the Eiger, the walker reaches the Gletscherschlucht. This is a narrow gorge below the tail of the Unterer Grindelwaldgletscher (lower Grindelwald glacier), which disappears from sight into the high summits as a narrow strip of ice. Well-sited galleries cling to the rocky walls and can (for a fee) be followed to view the ravine at close quarters.

As there are one or two places beneath the Eigerwand open to rock falls, this walk is not recommended after periods of heavy rain, or early in the season when the upper snows are still melting.

The Route

□ Take the Kleine Scheidegg train from the Grund station as far as the Alpiglen halt.

□ Walk past the group of farms to the east, away from the station.

□ Take the right and upper of the two footpaths beyond the restaurant and follow a series of white-red-white waymarks.

Alpiglen is a good place to view the Eigerwand.

□ Climb uphill, across high alpine meadows, and then through belts of sparse pine woods to the first of the streams draining the lower slopes of the Eigerwand.

□ Cross the rocky stream bed and climb steeply through forest towards the lower crags of the Wandflühe.

☐ Cross the second stream and contour across the rocky, tree covered slope beyond.

☐ Move out on to open scree-covered slopes, crossing three more streams in quick succession.

Take extra care on this open ground; it is swept by avalanches in late winter and occasional rocks still fall throughout the year, especially after rain.

☐ Start to walk downhill into the forest and swing round the lower slopes of the Hörnli ridge.

☐ Cross the rocky treeless stone-filled gulley of the Schüssellauenen, and re-enter the forest.

☐ Follow the path along a tricky route winding its way through the Boneren crags.

☐ Beyond a foresters' hut, the path turns left, and leads steeply downhill along the crest of the Gletscherschlucht ravine.

☐ Turn right at the junction with the path above the Gletscherschlucht restaurant, then go steeply down into the ravine.

☐ Turn right along the galleried path, returning by the same route to continue alongside the Weisse (white) Lütschine river as far as the restaurant.

The deep ravine was carved, first by the glacier when it reached this point, then later by the torrent of melt water flowing from the tail of the wall of ice which can be seen beneath the Eiger and its near neighbour, the Fieschorner.

☐ Follow the Erlenpromenade track downhill through forested lower slopes away from the restaurant. Reach the valley road at the Sand campsite to end a short but memorable walk beneath the home of the mountain ogre (Eiger means ogre in German).

10¼ miles (16.5km), 5 hours. Strenuous — 1,684ft (513m), ascent.

Nature, in carving the shape of the alps in the Jungfrau region, gave us the stark north walls of the giants enclosing the south side of the Grindelwald basin. On the north side of the basin, the slopes are relatively easier and the summits much lower; they have an advantage which is soon obvious to the mountain walker. Above the treeline the slopes, though steep, are ideal for easy walking. The ridges are broad and accessible, and the few lines of rocky crags are easily breached by well designed paths. A high alpine lake sits like a jewel beneath the final slopes of Faulhorn.

Flower lovers, expert and tyro alike, will enjoy this walk, especially on the slopes leading down to the Bachalpsee lake, or on the ridge to the west of Faulhorn; both are unspoilt areas attracting the growth of a wide range of alpine flowers.

Using First, Europe's longest chair lift (it takes about one hour to reach the top station), helps the walker to reach the wide open spaces of the mountain zone beyond the tree level. Height gained by reaching the summit of the Faulhorn — 8,799ft (2,681m) is retained for as long as possible; nearly all the way to Gummihorn on the Schynige Platte where a funicular railway will carry you down to Interlaken at the end of the day.

Bachalpsee

The Route

□ Take the First chair lift to its upper station. Turn left, away from the restaurant, and follow the signposted and white-red-white waymarked path towards the Faulhorn. The path ascends the rocky crags of the Langenbalm.

□ Cross the rocky beds of four streams in the space of about $\frac{3}{4}$ mile (1.2km) on high grassy slopes of the Widderfeld.

□ Walk on a level course across the scree slopes of Bach Gummi.

Cross the Grossbach river and walk between the two smaller lakes to the Bachalpsee lake.

The lake fills a hollow made by a long dead glacier, and makes an attractive place to picnic, or simply rest and maybe photograph the view of the Wetterhorn. The valley below the lake looks to the south-east directly towards the Wetterhorn, but the arm of the Simelihorn shuts out the view to the south. It will be necessary to wait until you reach the top of Faulhorn before the main panorama can be seen.

□ Climb west, then north, on stony ground, sometimes on bare rock and sometimes over scree, as far as the summit of the Faulhorn.

The last section is steep and can be circumvented by using a lower path beneath the summit, if you are not happy about the scramble involved in gaining the final few hundred feet.

There is a small alpine restaurant on the summit which provides shelter and sustenance, but the main reason for reaching it is the panoramic views it offers of all the nearby mountains and the peaks of the Jungfrau massif.

□ Follow the west ridge, downhill, around the heads of a series of side valleys. The path is rocky and sometimes leads across the top of a line of steep crags, but it is safe and well-made.

□ Ignore the paths right and left and follow signposts and waymarking towards the Schynige Platte.

□ Below the Laucherhorn — 7,319ft (2,230m) — the path leaves the ridge and descends easily, more or less south-west to the high alpine farms of Oberberg on the Schynige Platte.

□ Continue past Oberberg to Gummihorn and then to the upper station of the Interlaken-Schynige Platte railway on this high plateau. Take the Interlaken train to Wilderswil to connect with the Grindelwald train back up the Lütschine valley.

8 miles (13km). 5 hours. Moderate/strenuous — 2,340ft (713m), ascent.

Restaurant Stieregg is situated in a green mountain hollow, beneath the Schreckhorn and the mighty Eiger. To reach this spot it is necessary to follow a steep but well-made footpath through the upper section of the glacial ravine, draining the mighty cirque of rock and ice at its head. The path follows a route which has been carved from the rock, and in some places it works its way through open galleries to reach easier ground around the restaurant.

There are views from Stieregg directly out on to the ice falls of the lower Grindelwald glacier, with the Schreckhorn and Eiger to the left and right respectively. A connecting ridge between the two peaks blocks the exit from the upper glacier.

The Route

□ The walk starts at the road bridge beyond the Gletscherdorf campsite. Cross the river, away from the campsite and bear left away from the road.

□ Walk beneath the Pfingstegg cable car and follow the track, roughly parallel to the river, across the farmland and sparse forest as far as the farmhouses and villas at Auf der Sulz.

□ Following yellow waymarks and the signpost to Pfingstegg, walk uphill; first through the forest, then across open meadows to the scattered settlements of Obere Sulz.

□ Follow the path steeply uphill through a gap between the two belts of pine forest.

□Turn right beneath a series of crags to follow a level path as far as the Pfingstegg restaurant.

The timber restaurant will make a good break after the steep pull from Grindelwald. The view from the terrace includes the whole of the surrounding Grindelwald basin and the valley of the Schwarze Lütschine. To the left is the mouth of Gletscherschlucht ravine, with the Weisse (white) Lütschine living up to its descriptive name as it thunders down to join the main river.

□ Follow the Stieregg footpath (signposted from above the Pfingstegg restaurant) and waymarked in the white-red-white of mountain tracks.

□ The track climbs steadily in and out of craggy outcrops, above the treeline, following a cleverly-engineered route above the Gletscherschlucht ravine.

As the path begins to climb above the narrow confines of the ravine, the view, which hitherto has been of the Gletscherschlucht, opens slowly to reveal the jagged ice falls and terminal moraines of the glacier's tail. Beyond, rocky crags, worn smooth by the grinding of ice passing over them for thousands of years, protude from the steep middle section of the Unterer Grindelwald glacier.

□ Take care when crossing the Hohternenlamm stream draining from one of the western combes beneath the Wetterhorn.

The last ½ mile (800m) beyond the stream is over terminal moraines marking the limits the glacier reached before it, with the rest of alpine glaciers, shrank to its present size. This shrinkage still continues.

□ Continue, steeply in places, as far as the Stieregg restaurant.

□ Return by the same path as far as the first footpath junction above the Gletscherschlucht.

□ Turn left, then right, at the next junction.

□ Walk downhill away from the rocky ground and into forest.

□ Join the track from the Marmorbruch gasthof (refreshments) and turn right through farmland and alpine meadows to return to the road bridge which also marks the finish of this walk.

The Grindelwald Glacier, the Wetterhorn and the Schreckhorn

7 miles (11.3km), 8 hours. Strenuous — 3,571ft (1,088m) ascent.

This walk, like Walk 4, is along the side of a giant glacier, in this case it is Oberer (higher or upper) Grindelwaldgletscher. However, here the similarity ends, for this is a walk of real mountaineering proportions. The amount of climbing involved is much greater and the path is a lot steeper and rockier, but the rewards are therefore more appreciated.

The route, which starts at the eastern end of the Grindelwald basin, climbs rapidly by the Ischpfad path across the lower slopes of the Krinnenhörner — 8,983ft (2,737m), the northern and higher partner of the Weisshorn — 7,621ft (2,322m). Turning a corner created by a western spur of the Krinnenhörner, the mountain walker gets his first glimpse of the Oberer Grindelwald glacier. Following remains of its lateral or side moraines, the path begins its final and steepest climb, beneath the slopes of the Weisshorn, to the Swiss Alpine Club's Gleckstein hut.

This walk is only suitable for experienced mountain walkers.

The Route

□ Take the valley bus as far as the Wetterhorn Hotel at the eastern end of Grindelwald.

□ Walk up the Grosse Scheidegg road to the group of farms at the Unter Lauchbühl.

□ Turn right, away from the road, at the signpost to the Glecksteinhütte SAC.

□ Climb a small rise through a pine wood and then walk down to the Gutzbach stream.

□ Cross the stream to follow the white-red-white mountain path waymarks of the Ischpfad path.

□ The path now begins to climb in earnest up the lower slopes of the Byhorn, at 7,119ft (2,169m); a satellite of the Krinnenhörner.

Take special care on exposed sections of the path. Above it towers the impossibly steep walls of the mountain giants.

□ Around the western spur the angle of the climb eases slightly, but it is only a temporary respite.

The view below is of the crevassed glacier and the eye is drawn upwards through a scene of chaos to the smooth pure white snows of the summit ridges.

☐ Follow the path across the scree and moraine slopes, broken only by rocky spurs to the Weisshorn.

☐ Climb through layers of crags at Schlupf by steep zigzags.

☐ The hardest climbing continues for only about 800yd (732m), but it will take almost an hour to cover the distance between Schlupf and Schönbühl.

☐ The final stretch as far as the hut is on comparatively easy ground.

If this is your first visit to an alpine hut, you will be struck immediately by the simple but friendly atmosphere which is found, to a greater or lesser degree, in all mountain huts. The hut, owned by the Swiss Alpine Club, offers food and accommodation to anyone; however members of the SAC get preferential terms.

The hut is in a magnificent situation, with unsurpassed views of mountain splendour. It is used by climbers attempting the peaks of the Weisshorn massif.

☐Return by the same route, but take care on the steep downhill sections, especially those on loose rock or scree slopes.

Even though the return is along the same path as the outward journey, the views are just as interesting, being from a different angle. Also you will feel more inclined to appreciate the views, not having to put so much effort into walking downhill!

THE GRINDELWALD BASIN
(a walk for a rainy day)

---

10 miles (6km), 4 hours. Easy/moderate.

Hard though it may seem, it could rain during your walking holiday in Grindelwald. Even though this will probably mean that plans for high-level walking for the day have to be abandoned, it does not mean that walking has to be completely shelved.

No doubt the streets and shops of this glacier village, as it likes to be known, have already been investigated, but the fields and riverside around the locality can still be explored. This walk can therefore be reserved for either a day when a gentle stroll is more attractive than a steep climb, or for a day when low clouds and rain prevent higher exploration.

The route follows the main street out past the church into fields planted with fruit trees, or over open pasture. The only climb of note is beyond the moraine at the foot of the Oberer Grindelwald glacier to the Milchbach restaurant. The rest of the walk is downhill, more or less alongside the river, in and out of pine forest and across the meadows as far as a convenient railway station for the return journey by train.

The beauty of this walk is that it can be extended or cut short almost at will, depending on the day or the mood of the party.

The Route

□ From the centre of Grindelwald, walk east along the busy main street as far as the church.

□ Take the left fork along the Grosse Scheidegg road for about 550yd (503m) and turn right on a yellow waymarked footpath, down past a group of buildings to the tree-shrouded stream below.

□ Walk through meadows over a slight rise, then down to the Horbach river.

□ Turn left and follow the river upstream as far as the road.

□ Turn right along the road, following it over the Bergelbach river as far as the Wetterhorn hotel.

□ Turn right opposite the hotel, cross the river and climb up through a belt of trees keeping to a wide gravel-surfaced track.

□ Walk across an open space filled with rocks and rubble brought down by melt-water from the Oberer Grindelwald glacier.

This rock-strewn area is known as Gletchersand. Originally it marked a terminal moraine of the Oberer Grindelwald glacier, but it is now filled with rocks and gravel brought down by floodwater from the melting glacier. Occasional avalanches at the end of winter have also added their contribution to this wilderness.

□ Climb by either of two paths which zigzag up the steep hillside to the Milchbach restaurant, perched on the Halsegg, is an impudent little spur which juts out from the foot of the Schreckhorn.

□ Walk away from the restaurant and take the right-hand of two paths diverging along an outcrop of crags, 250yd (229m) to the south-west.

Take care if descending this rocky section in the wet; it will be very slippery.

□ Walk downhill along the upper edge of a pine wood and across a rocky slope as far as the main river.

□ Turn left downstream, at first in forest, and later along a farm road as far as the Gletscherdorf campsite.

□ Cross the river and immediately turn left past the campsite, along the side lane as far as the glacier restaurant.

□ Go left on to the road and parallel to the railway, but do not go as far as Grund station.

□ Cross the Kleine Scheidegg mountain railway line and almost immediately turn left over the river on a side road.

□ Take the right fork and follow the road past the Eigernordwand campsite.

□ Take the right fork at the bottom of the Aspen ski tow.

□ Walk through meadows, passing little farms along the track, which now follows the river at the foot of a tree-covered rocky spur.

□ Continue downstream on the left bank of the river, through natural pine forest as far as Burglauenen. Cross over the river and into the village to catch the train back to Grindelwald.

It is possible to continue downstream, avoiding the main road, by using side lanes and footpaths for 6 or 7 miles (9.6 or 11.3km) towards Zweilütschinen above Interlaken, in the lower Lütschine valley.

If using this extension try to plan the route to coincide with a convenient station for the return journey to Grindelwald.

KANDERSTEG

Maps

Landeskarte der Schweiz (1: 50,000 series) sheet 263 — Wildstrubel and sheet 264 — Jungfrau. Or Kandersteg Wanderkarte (1: 25,000) produced by the Kandersteg Tourist Office. (Verkersverein Kandersteg, CH 3718).

How to get there:

Road:
1   South through Basel and Bern to Spiez. Valley road south to Kandersteg.
2   Black Forest route to Schaffhausen, then south-west via Zürich, Lucerne and Spiez.

Rail:
Main line via Bern and south by the Lötschberg line to Kandersteg.

Air:
International airports at Bern and Zürich, with rail connections.

The Area

With the creation of a car transporter service on trains running south through the Lötschberg tunnel to Brig, or to Domodossola in Italy, the valley road carries rather more traffic than one would expect. Fortunately this well-made road by-passes Kandersteg, and even though the middle and lower valley can sometimes be congested, the roads around Kandersteg are relatively quiet.

The Kander valley flows more or less north, draining a massive wall of mountains, ranging from the Blüemlisalp to the Balmhorn in the west, and cut only by the Lötschberg tunnel. Most of the water to feed the main and side valleys comes from the melting Kander glacier, with others which are smaller, but which hang with awesome majesty from high points on this wall.

Because it sits on a high plateau at the valley head, Kandersteg is favoured by a better than average amount of sunshine; the mountain wall to the south causes most of the rain bearing clouds to empty before they reach the valley.

Kandersteg has long been a walkers' paradise, where there is something for everyone, from the serious alpinist to parents who want to introduce a young family to the delights of mountain scenery. Situated at around 3,850ft (1,176m), and connected by chairlifts and cable cars to a series of high-level, easy walking areas, Kandersteg is an ideal place for anyone who cannot, or does not want to climb steep hillsides. Well graded footpaths follow easy contours across the hillsides and pleasant lakeside tracks or forest walks have produced one of the easiest walking centres in the alps. There are over 220 miles (350km) of well marked paths in the area, which should be more than enough to satisfy everyone's needs.

Sunnbüel is aptly named. Reached by a cable car from Eggeschwand, a mile or so up the valley from Kandersteg, this sunny bowl is just made for lazy rambling. There is a restaurant at the upper station of the Sunnbüel lift and an alpine hut on the summit of the Gemmipass, for those with energy to walk an extra mile or so beyond Sunnbühl's high-level lake.

Two other and better known lakes are nearby. One is reached by a chairlift from Kandersteg; this is the Oeschinensee, filling a hole carved thousands of years ago by a long dead glacier. Pine forests clothe its western shore and steep cliffs drop sheer to its eastern limits. This romantic setting is the place for a picnic before following one of the easy footpaths back to Kandersteg. Tiny Blausee, the so aptly named 'blue lake' is a natural phenomenon set in a small nature reserve. The deep blue colouring of this lake is thought to come from algae living in the clear waters, and not from chemical action deep within the earth as was once thought.

There are plenty of other activities in and around the district, from an all the year skating rink to tennis, and in the evenings there is entertainment with a local flavour in local hotels and bars. Ivory carving is something of a local craft, with pieces offered for sale in village shops.

Useful Information

Local Tourist Office

Verkehrsbüro Kandersteg
CH 3718 — Kandersteg
Telephone: 033 75 1234

Accommodation

From five star hotels to rented accommodation. Dormitory accommodation for groups or individuals, and two campsites.

Mountain Railway

Lötschberg line from Spiez to Brig.

Kandersteg and the Kandertal, with the Balmhorn

Cable Car and Chair Lifts

Kandersteg — Oeschinensee (chair)
Eggeschwand — Sunnbüel (cabin and chair)
Stechelburg — Schilthorn (above Lauterbrunnen) (cabin)

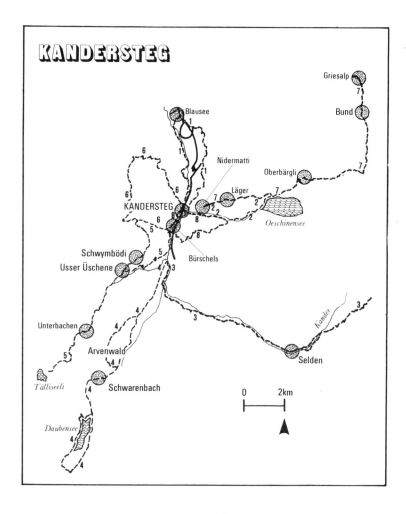

7½ miles (12km), 3-4 hours. Easy/moderate.

This is a good way of getting to know Kandersteg and the surrounding valley. At the climax of the walk, the Blue Lake appears almost as though it has been conjured up by a magician. The unbelievably deep blue of its crystal clear waters make it look as though it has been artifically coloured. However, this is not so; the colour is completely natural, even though its origin is still open to question.

The lake is home to massive alpine trout, which can be seen swimming in the clear water. The fish are also bred nearby at a commercial trout farm — a point worth remembering by anyone on a self-catering holiday, for the trout are on sale. Other creatures bred near the Blue Lake are Saint Bernard dogs, always a popular attraction with children. It is possible to see submerged petrified tree stumps from boat trips on the lake. These are relics of a time before the lake came into being. A terrace restaurant, overlooking the lake, completes highlights of an introductory walk around the Kander valley.

From the village, the route of the walk is through the village and then a short climb past the ski jump leads into pine woods, where an easy path leads down to Mitholz. The Blausee is less than a mile away. On the return, a path which follows the west bank of the Kander river is used to reach Kandersteg.

The Route

☐ Leave Kandersteg by following the old road north-east through the hamlet of Nidermatti.

☐ At point 1173 turn right through woodland as far as a path junction.

☐ Turn left and pass beneath the ski jump platforms.

☐ Climb steadily through pine forest, until an open area caused by winter avalanches is reached.

☐ Contour below the pine forest across a rough area. Walk over steep alpine meadows then re-enter the forest.

The avalanche zone, and open meadowland nearby, is a good area to look for alpine flowers; also occasional deer may be seen briefly, flitting through the woods.

☐ Climb higher to point 1269 and then turn left slightly downhill to an area of dwarf pines. The stunting is caused by occasional winter avalanches which sweep the lower slopes of Bire — 8,212ft (2,502m). Cross a stream and return to the forest.

☐ Fork left, downhill, at a path junction inside the forest. Follow this path beneath mature pines to the Stegen stream.

☐ Cross the mountain stream and begin to walk steeply downhill into Mitholz.

☐ Follow the main road for about ⅓ mile (541m) and then leave it by turning right on a narrow lane. Cross a series of fields by this lane and then go under the railway line.

The railway at this point loses height in a series of massive loops, some of which are underground.

☐ Cross more fields and then go left over the main road to reach the Blausee, which will be signposted away from the main road.

The Blausee makes an obvious picnic spot and could be used to finish the walk with the rest of the route saved for another day. If this should be the case, then return by either train or bus from Mitholz.

The Return Route

☐ Walk away from the lake back to the road and turn right along it, then right again after ⅓ mile (541m).

☐ Follow a farm road to the right, south-west down to the river.

☐ Cross the river by a wooden bridge and walk forwards to a track junction.

☐ Turn left on a valley track which roughly parallels the river. Follow it upstream through meadows and stretches of shady forest.

☐ Beyond the farm Underem Büel, the track climbs uphill to a series of small farms at Ägerte.

☐ From Ägerte, a footpath follows the wide brow of the forested hillside to link with a minor road leading directly to Kandersteg station. Watch out for traffic approaching and leaving the car terminus. The main village is at the top of the station approach.

5 miles (8km). Using the chair lift — 2½ hours. Easy.

A walker visiting the Kandersteg area without including a trip to the Oeschinensee lake is missing an experience which could be the highlight of the holiday. Anyone not able to walk long distances or at high altitude and yet wishes to get the feel of the mountains, can experience this from a visit to the lake. At Oeschinensee, there is a real feeling of being amongst the giants of the alps; the mountains are so near and yet the effort of reaching the lake is negligible. A chair lift whisks the visitor from the outskirts of Kandersteg to the lake at the moderate altitude of 5,179ft (1,578m). A gentle path leads down from the upper station, over alpine meadows then through shady pine woods before reaching a restaurant by the lake shore. Peaks rise up majestically, with almost vertical slopes starting directly from the lake.

This is a walk for an off day, or perhaps for a day when it is too hot for any of the more ambitious tours. If a picnic beneath a shady tree close to the lake or perhaps a swim is more suitable, this trip is designed with those possibilities in mind.

On the return journey, either use the chair lift back or follow a cool path downhill through the forest alongside the Oeschinenbach river.

The Route

□ Use the Kandersteg — Oeschinensee chair lift to reach the lake. The bottom station is to the east of the village and close to the campsite.

□ Walk away from the upper station, following the signposted track across alpine meadows, contouring on a level course as far as a small stream.

□ Turn right downhill to the farm building at Läger.

It is not possible to walk right round the lake, but one can explore as far as is safe on both sides. There are alpine trout in Oeschinensee and fishing is permitted between 15 June and 30 September; check locally about permits. There are also rowing boats for hire.

□ Walk to the lakeside and turn right following the woodland path to the restaurant and hotel.

□ Turn right away from the restaurant and follow the signposted path downhill into the Oeschinenbach valley. At first the path crosses a series of open meadows, and then gradually trees crowd in to make a shady route down the valley.

□ Follow the course of the stream.

□ At a junction of paths, turn left and cross the stream.

□ Climb slightly — still in the forest, and then across an open avalanche zone.

□ The rest of the way to Kandersteg is down a gentle forested slope. Above the open farmland and yet close to the village there is a choice of three routes; take whichever will bring you closest to your holiday location.

Path to the Oeschinensee above Kandersteg. Blüemlisalp in the background.

To Selden (returning by bus) — 10 miles (16km), 5 hours. Easy.
To Kanderfirn (returning by bus) — 14 miles (23km), 7-8 hours.
Strenuous (above Selden).

This is a beautiful walk which reaches into the heart of the mountains, yet with the help of the minibus service to Selden, one can return to the lower valley without the necessity for either a long walk or an overnight stay in a high-level hotel or mountain hut.

This is a walk for all the family, for no matter what their abilities, most walkers can at least reach the central part of the valley. The height difference between Kandersteg and Selden is 1,172ft (357m), and from Selden to the bottom of the Kanderfirn glacier is another 2,868ft (874m), making a total of 4,040ft (1,231m) of climbing from Kandersteg. The second section is therefore a tough climb, but one which will reward the walker with tremendous views of the terrifying jaws at the end of a glacier. Above the glacier stretches a blue and white wilderness of snow and ice, broken only by the sinister lines of partly covered crevasses.

On the way up to Selden, walkers will be treated to a natural display of alpine flowers growing in this remarkable setting. Gentian and asters are common, but that rarity, the ladies-slipper orchid, can occasionally be found in damp shady spots. Please remember, it is illegal to pick these flowers in Switzerland!

Check details of bus services locally and if possible try to book seats beforehand.

The Route

□ Take the valley bus from Kandersteg to the Eggeschwand campsite.

□ Turn left away from the forest, crossing the Kander river. Then join the Gasteretal road on rocky ground near the lower road tunnel.

This minor road, serving the Gasteretal valley, is a good example of the trouble taken by the Swiss to provide access to a comparatively remote valley.

□ Walk along the gravel-surfaced road for about ¼ mile (400m), with the river carving the deep Chluse gorge on the left.

□ Where the road turns left across the river, keep straight on along a signposted track to the Waldhus restaurant.

□ Take the left fork beyond the restaurant and follow the river until a bridge crossing regains the valley road. Turn right along this road following it as far as Selden.

There are optional paths on the opposite side of the valley which can be reached, away from the road, by turning at signposts. Follow either the road or footpaths to Selden and its cluster of hotels.

Selden is a typical alpine summer farm settlement where animals are still brought from farms in the lower valley every year. Some of the farms have been developed into basic hotels and restaurants.

A decision must be made at Selden, either to spend the rest of the day picnicking and exploring this middle section of Gasteretal before returning by minibus, or to continue along the valley as far as the glacier. If the latter is chosen, then the following directions apply.

□ Beyond Selden the valley road ends and a track, gradually narrowing into a footpath, climbs steadily to Berghaus Heimritz, a comfortable little gasthof with simple accommodation.

□ Follow the (true) right bank of the Kander river, above the treeline and on increasingly rocky ground as far as point 1724.

□ Cross the stream and turn left, up an increasingly steep path over rough ground, made from debris of the terminal moraine of the retreating Kanderfirn glacier.

□ As the angle of ascent steepens, the path begins to zigzag to follow the easiest course available.

□ Do not go on to the terminal icefall of the glacier, but end the climbing part of the walk where you can obtain the best view.

The Kanderfirn is just one of a massive system of glaciers surrounding the peaks of the Tschingelhorn – 11,740ft (3,577m), and the Breithorn – 12,413ft (3,782m). The Petersgrat ridge forms the southern wall on the right as you look up the glacier. To the north are the complex ridges of the Blüemlisalp range.

□ Return almost to point 1724, but do not cross the stream. Follow the left bank of the Kander until the path changes sides above Selden. Here, there should just be sufficient time for a drink and maybe something to eat before catching the minibus back to Kandersteg.

12 miles (19.3km), 8-9 hours. Moderate — 1,601ft (488m) ascent.

Sunnbüel is aptly named; it means 'sun bowl' and, providing the weather is kind, this high-level hollow beneath the peaks forms a real sun trap.

The walk described below can be split into sections to suit everyone. The lower valley, between the Sunnbüel chair lift and the pretty lakes at Spittelmatte and Arvenseeli, provides an easy walk designed for rambling and for appreciating the natural beauty of the area. Above Spittelmatte the path crosses a natural alpine rock garden, to reach the partially man-made lake of Daubensee, at 7,240ft (2,206m). Beyond, the path steepens, to climb the Gemmi Pass — 7,621ft (2,322m), a narrow gap in the rocky ridge between Plattenhörner, a subsidiary ridge of the Rinderhorn — 11,333ft (3,453m) and the Daubenhorn — 9,656ft (2,942m).

Access to Sunnbüel is easy; the first stage is by the Stock cable car which climbs steeply into the north-eastern end of the 'bowl'; next a chairlift rides the half-mile into a more open area on the edge of Spittelmatte.

The Route

□ Use the Stock cable car, followed by the Sunnbüel chairlift, to reach the walking area in the upper valley.

□ Walk away from the chairlift in a southerly direction, across gently sloping alpine meadows as far as the twin lakes of Spittlematte.

It will be necessary to divert to the right, away from the path, in order to explore these two tiny lakes, but the diversion will be worthwhile.

□ Turn right at point 1875, joining the track from Stock to the Gemmipass.

A little way above the junction with the Stock track, a series of waymarked paths leads off to the right, around the wooded area of Arvenwald. The flora of this area is particularly good in early summer. Anyone not wishing to climb all the way to the top of the pass could spend an enjoyable hour or so wandering through the Arvenwald woods, and perhaps meeting up with the rest of their group at the Schwarenbach restaurant later in the day.

◻ Walk up the boulder-strewn hillside, which gets gradually steeper, to the Schwarenbach restaurant.

◻ Climb from the restaurant across rocky ground to lake Daubensee.

◻ Follow the east shore of the lake and climb away from it on a well-designed path which climbs all the way to the summit of the Gemmipass.

Below the summit restaurant, the view is directly onto the high-altitude spa of Leukerbad at the end of a valley of a tributary of the Rhône.

◻ Return by way of a path which drops steeply into the Lämmerendalu ravine and turn right over rocky ground, following the stream to the west shore of the Daubensee.

◻ Follow the shoreline path until it joins the path which was used to climb the Gemmipass. Turn left and walk down into Sunnbüel by way of Schwarenbach.

◻ At the path junction near Spittelmatte turn left to reach the upper chair lift station.

An option would be to turn right at point 1,875 and walk partly in shady forest to the Stock lift, thus omitting the chair lift.

Hiking near Kandersteg

12 miles (19.3km),5-6 hours. Moderate/strenuous — 2,232ft (680m) ascent.

Several walks and climbs can be made from the upper station of the Kandersteg-Allmenalp cabin lift. This walk, and the next, are just two of the possibilities the lift offers alpine walkers and scramblers.

The walk crosses high Allmenalp, where in summer, local farmers graze their cattle and make cheese from the milk. Visitors to Allmenalp are welcome to watch the process of cheese-making, especially if they buy some form of refreshment, or cheese. Beyond the alp, the track contours easily beneath the rocky slopes of the Chlyne Lohner ridges (*chlyne* is the local spelling of *kleiner* — small or little) until it reaches the Üschene farming valley and the Alpbach stream. Here an easy track, used as access to the high summer pasture, climbs steadily towards the valley head. A steep but comparatively short path climbs another 1,313ft (400m), through a gap in the surrounding crags to reach Lake Tälliseeli. The lake is fed by waters draining from the Tälli glacier, filling the high combe beneath the Roter Totz — 9,321ft (2,840m), and the Steghorn —10,325ft (3,146m).

Tälliseeli lake is the climax of the walk in more than one sense. Its dramatic situation beneath the frowning crags of the Engstliglengrat ridge, and the Steghorn/Roter Totz combe make it a memorable target.

The Route

□ Reach Allmenalp by cable car from Kandersteg.

□ Turn left away from the upper station and follow the marked (white-red-white) path towards Üschene.

Cheese-making can be watched at summer farms on Allmenalp. Check locally for times etc. Refreshments available.

□ Follow a wide path south-west over two streams and across sparsely-wooded rocky alpine meadows.

□ Ignore lesser paths to the right and left, and still following the main path, contour round and into the Üschene valley.

□ Beyond the farmstead of Ryharts, the path improves, still following a level course in and out of sparse pine forest.

□ Descend gradually into the valley and its access road, which is joined at Usser Üschene.

The high Üschene valley, with the Alpbach river, holds typical summer pasture which has been used by generations of farmers from the main valley. The process of bringing animals here from their over-wintering at home farms is known as 'transhumance'.

□ Turn right along the valley road and climb steadily alongside the river, past the farmsteads of Uf der Egge, as far as the road end at Unterbächen.

□ Bear left at point 1897 away from the gravel-surfaced road, and begin the steepest part of the climb.

□ The path crosses a series of streams draining through rocky ground below the surrounding peaks.

□ The natural gap in the craggy bastion at Walliswang gives final access over glacier-worn slabs, to Lake Tälliseeli.

Try to reach the lake with plenty of time in hand, in order to really appreciate its setting.

□ Return by the same route as far as Usser Üschene. Turn right to follow the valley access road down to Kandersteg.

□ The gravel road leaves the comparatively level middle valley to plunge, by a series of steep zigzags, across the pine clad slopes of the upper Kander valley.

□ Short cuts away from the road can be made to the left and downhill, towards Filfalle where, at the scout camp, a bus can be caught to save the final mile or so of road walking into Kandersteg.

---

6 miles (9.6km), 6 hours. Strenuous — 2,701ft (823m) ascent

This, the second walk from Kandersteg/Allmenalp cable car, is a truly exhilerating high-level alpine outing for both novices and experienced mountaineers alike.

Two summits are crossed on this route; both are sharp-pointed and meet everyone's expectation of what a real mountain should be like! The route climbs the steep south-east face of the Allmegrat ridge by a series of sweeping zigzags to reach the final ridge up to the First peak — 8,366ft (2,549m). In order to avoid the narrow ridges across Howang, the route drops beneath its western face, across broken rocky ground to follow a fairly easy track to Stand — 7,614ft (2,320m). The steep north-west ridge off Stand needs more care than usual, but once the walker is on the high col of the Golitschenhörni, the going gets progressively easier. The path follows the easiest ground available and works its way around the main valley's lower crags before dropping through forest back into Kandersteg.

NB: Some words of warning are necessary to anyone considering this fine walk. Make sure that you are well equipped for this high-altitude mountaineering route (see the Introductory chapter for details of clothing, fitness, etc). Also, please do not attempt to cross any steep snowfields, unless all your party are carrying ice axes and know how to use them. Check locally in case there is any snow forecast.

The Route

☐ Follow the First signpost away from the upper station of the cable car. The route is marked with red stripes on a white blocked background.

☐ Climb steadily in a westerly direction across high alpine pasture.
The sheltered combe of Obere Allme should be an excellent area for alpine flowers in early summer.

☐ Turn right, to the north-east, above the farm building of Obere Allme and begin the steady climb towards First.

☐ Turn left at an old building at point 2027, then gradually swing right, still climbing, on rocky ground.

□ The final 771ft (235m) of the First climb starts at a crossing with an old path. This is the steepest part of the ascent, but gradually the summit comes into view above its side ridges.

Look all around from the top of First and try to identify as many of the surrounding giants as possible. Those to the east include the Jungfrau and the Eiger; Mont Blanc and its satellites are to the south-west, with the Matterhorn and Monte Rosa to the south. Before setting off on the next stage of the route, make sure that the path is clear and snow is not blocking the north side of the ridge.

It is unwise and hazardous not to retreat in the face of dangerous conditions on a mountain.

□ Cross easier ground on a contouring path and then climb the broad south-west ridge to the top of Stand.

□ Follow with great care the short but steep north-west ridge away from Stand.

□ Bear right on a contouring path as far as the col and turn right across the grassy hillside of Golitschenhörni.

□ Zigzag downhill over steep rocky ground to point 1833.

□ Contour towards, then steeply down to and across, a stream.

□ Follow the path around the shoulder, meeting the first sparse pines of the forest and hillside.

□ Keep a sharp lookout for the waymarking red on white symbols across the high boulderfield, and descend to a junction of paths at point 1337.

□ Take the central of three paths, south-east, downhill through forest and enter Kandersteg $\frac{1}{4}$ mile (400m) to the north of the railway station.

(From the Oeschinen chair lift to the Gornergrund valley road end). 10 miles (16km). 9 hours. Strenuous — 4,306ft (1,312m) ascent.

The most sensible way to do this walk is to take two days. Stay at the Swiss Alpine Club's Blüemlisalphütte, — 9,302ft (2,834m) — and split nine hours of tough walking into two comparatively easy days.

To those who have never stayed in an alpine hut, perhaps a word of explanation is necessary. To many English-speaking people, the word 'hut' calls up a mental picture of a small and inconvenient wooden shack. Some huts in the high regions of Switzerland are tiny stone-built affairs, but most (and Blüemlisalphütte is one) are sturdy buildings offering simple accommodation and wholesome food at moderate prices. In other words a hut is a basic high-level hotel, offering food and shelter to anyone walking in the mountains. There is no need to book in advance, and while there are privilege rates for club members, one night at this hut would not warrant joining the Swiss Alpine Club.

The route from the chair lift climbs quickly and smoothly above the Oeschinen lake, reaching the bare rocks and screes of the world of the true mountaineer. The hut itself is perched above the Blüemlisalp glacier which tumbles down from the snows of the Morgenhorn, Wyssi Frau and the Blüemlisalphorn itself. By getting up early next morning you will experience a light which can only be seen in the high mountains. A narrow ridge separating two snowfields leads down to the summer farms of Bund; from here an easy walk reaches the valley.

This is a really exceptional high-level walk so make sure that you are well equipped for the expedition. Also check the times of the postbuses down the Kiental valley from Gries, in order to plan the walk down from the hut.

The walk could be completed in one day by hard walkers, but they would have to plan their transport arrangements very carefully as it is a long way back from Gries to Kandersteg.

The Route

☐ Leave the Oeschinen chair lift and walk down to the north shore of the lake.

☐ Climb away from the lake through an area of rocks and old glacier debris to the Underbärglialp.

There is a good view of the lake from Underbärglialp.

☐ Climb by zigzags to the high farms at Oberbärgli and join a path climbing from the left.

☐ Turn right away from the farms to follow a narrow mountain stream. Walk on the path away from the high pasture towards rockier ground.

This is a good area for alpine flowers. Chamois and marmots may also be seen, although possibly only the whistle of the latter may be heard.

☐ The final stage of about 1½ miles (2.4km) to the hut is steep and the ground is scree-covered and rocky, so take time and care.

The hut is perched on a broad ridge between two glaciers, and the Wildi Frau – 10,699ft (3,260m) makes the stern foreground to snow-covered ridges beyond. Red legged choughs and possibly buzzards are likely to be the only birds at this altitude. The scenery around the hut is magnificent and should be enjoyed at leisure; do not hurry.

☐ Next morning, before the sun gets too hot, walk back down the track for about 200yd (183m) and turn right at the signposted junction to Bund and Gornergrund.

☐ Walk down the ridge on a rough and rocky track which gradually improves as the path loses height.

☐ Bear left on the main path, ignoring the side paths, until you reach a group of farmsteads at Bund.

☐ Walk through the settlement and down into the main valley. Turn left along the valley track to reach the road end.

☐ Walk along the road for about ¾ mile (1.2km) and catch the postbus from Gries. It will drop you in the Kander valley where another bus, or the train, will complete this memorable tour.

4½ miles (7.2km), 3-3½ hours. Moderate — 1,136ft (346m) ascent.

This is a walk for days when it rains in the morning and then improves too late to consider any of the higher routes. Alternatively it can be used to fill the last few hours before leaving this delightful part of the upper Kander valley.

The path moves away from the main village, parallel to the railway and across scented meadows. The climb on the opposite side of the valley is steep, but once this is completed the walking is easy and the views are wide. Most of the routes described around Kandersteg can be seen from the walk and they will bring back happy memories as you move around and above the village.

The Route

☐ Walk down the street towards the station and cross to the west side of the tracks.

☐ Turn left and follow the railway through meadows as far as the road from the Almenalp lift.

☐ Turn left beneath the railway and immediately right along a side path, passing Hotel Ruedihaus on the way.

☐ Cross the main road and follow the lane towards Hotel Doldenhorn.

☐ Bear right, away from the hotel's access drive, and aim towards the lower edge of the pine forest.

☐ Turn left into the forest and climb steeply on a zigzag path to the slopes of Biberg.

☐ Bear left at the junction with the Doldenhorn Hut path.

☐ Still in deep forest, climb the final 500yd (457m) on to the little hilltop of Biberg.

Biberg is an excellent viewpoint for the lower valley and its surrounding peaks.

☐ Keep straight on at a junction with a second Doldenhorn path.

☐ Take care on the final steep descent into the Oeschinen valley.

☐ Left at the junction with the valley path, and follow it downhill all the way to Kandersteg.

If time allows and you feel up to it, make a diversion around the Vita Parcours (keep fit course) on the left of the valley track.

OBERGOMS (CONCHES VALLEY) — VALAIS

Maps

Landeskarte der Schweiz (1:50,000 series) Sheet 265 — Nufenenpass, and Sheet 264 — Jungfrau. The local tourist board also issue an excellent footpath map (1:50,000) based on the Swiss National Survey.

How to get there:

Road:

1 South by the European motorway network to Zürich, then via Zug or Lucerne to Altdorf and Andermatt. South-west over the Furka and Grimsel Passes into the Goms Valley.

2 Via Geneva, Lausanne and Martigny to Brig, then north-east along the Goms Valley.

Rail:

Main line Trans-European (Italian Services) to Brig. Transfer to the rack and pinion train for the Goms Valley resorts. **NB:** this train starts outside the main line station at Brig.

Air:

International airports at Bern and Geneva. Rail connections via Brig.

The Area

This is the valley of the infant Rhône, famed for its vintages in its lower reaches, but here in the Obergoms it is well above the maximum altitude for viniculture. This is true alpine country; the river starts its life draining the mighty Rhône glacier, but within a couple of miles is tamed as it flows through the high alpine farmland of Obergoms.

Three famous road passes — the Grimsel, Furka, and Nufenen

The summit of the Furka Pass

— all above 7,000ft (2,133m), lead out from the valley to make exciting driving, and a test for car and driver alike. The railway with its 'Glacier Express' which starts in Zermatt, climbs through the mountains in a complex system of tunnels and viaducts before reaching St Moritz, which makes it one of the most exciting railway rides in the world.

A line of old villages, spaced amongst the lush pastures, have been here for centuries. The uniquely-timbered barns, known as *Raccards* or *Mazots,* stand on their straddle-stones. They are built in this way to lift them above the heavy snow falls of winter and also to prevent rodent invasion.

Accommodation can be found in comfortable family-run hotels and guesthouses in most villages. Their cuisine caters for people with appetites sharpened by clean mountain air and healthy exercise.

Not so well known as the more popular alpine resorts, Obergoms has much to offer the walker who wants to explore new ground. An excellent footpath system, with carefully engineered gradients and easy to follow waymarkings will give everyone, from the slow and steady rambler to the more energetic hill walker, ample opportunity for more than a two weeks' stay in this valley. There is scope for hours of easy walking along the valley bottom, by tracks through meadows or on pine-clad lower hillsides. More ambitious walks above the treeline will be rewarded by views of the snow-clad peaks towering above the Obergoms.

Frequent trains, running with the efficiency of the Swiss railway system, make it possible to begin or end walks in most of the tiny villages throughout the length of the valley.

A series of linked footpaths, all with connecting tracks to and from villages, make up the 18¼ miles (29½km) Gommer Höhenweg. The walk, which can be done over any number of days using the train, starts at Bellwald and finishes at Oberwald. The route, which is on the north-west side of the valley and therefore enjoys maximum sunshine, is marked with a white-red-white block symbol.

Useful Information

Local Tourist Office
Verkehrsverein Münster,
CH 3985 Münster/Valais
Telephone: 028 73 1745

Accommodation
Ranges from small, family-run, inexpensive hotels to rented rooms. Details from the tourist office.

Campsites
Oberwald and Ulrichen.

Cable Cars and Chair Lifts
Panoramic views of the Aletsch Glacier and the south face of the Jungfrau and Eiger mountains.

Glacier Viewing
Rhône Glacier   From the Belvédère — Furka Pass. Do not miss the famous ice grotto and panorama of nearby peaks.
Aletsch Glacier   Cable car from Fiesch.
Gries Glacier   Above the Griesee lake. Access by footpath from the Nufenen Pass.

Rail Excursions on the 'Glacier Express'

It is possible to reach places as far apart as St Moritz or Zermatt using this unique train. Check timetables locally — some early services often use buses for part of the journey.

Road Passes

Grimsel	7,103ft (2,165m)
Furka	7,976ft (2,431m)
Nufenen	8,130ft (2,478m)

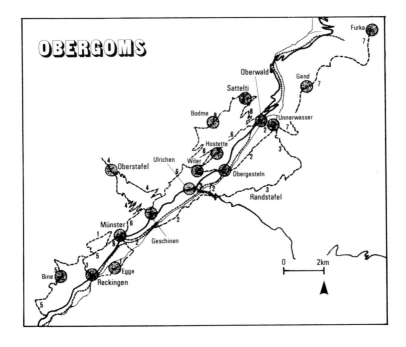

5 miles (8km), 2-2½ hours. Moderate. One steep uphill section.

This is a gentle ramble, ideal for the first day of the holiday, when muscles, cramped after travelling across Europe, do not want to be forced into energetic activity. It is also ideal for days when a morning's poor weather improves by lunchtime, or perhaps to fill the odd couple of hours or so at the end of a day spent doing other things.

The route passes through two of the most interesting villages in this high valley, where carefully-preserved farm buildings, built mainly of timber and resting on stones to prevent vermin from entering food stores, nestle into the landscape. Beyond the villages, easy paths take in both low and high-level pasture on the sunny west facing hillside. River and forest combine with open meadows to make this an ideal walk for a lazy day amidst the scenery of high alpine summits.

The Route

□ Take the train to Reckingen, or park close by in the village.

Turn right outside the station, and walk towards the river along a farm road. Cross the river by the bridge.

□ Immediately across the bridge the road divides. Take the left fork on to a cart track. Follow this alongside the river, through meadowland, for about 1¼ miles (2km), skirting the edge of a forest of mature pines until a group of farm buildings is reached at Eiget.

□ Turn left in front of the farm onto a rough road. Follow this over the river and climb up to Münster.

Münster village is a unique collection of carefully-preserved buildings, many of which have been here for centuries. The Baroque church with its 'candle-snuffer' spire is especially worth visiting; it has a fine altarpiece, dedicated to the Virgin, which was painted by a Lucerne artist in 1509.

Farmhouses on either side of the road into Münster will catch the eye, but probably the hospitable restaurants or the old post inn will offer the greatest attraction at midday.

□ Look for a footpath sign indicating the path to the Galmihornhütte.

Follow this signposted track, at first along the village street, then out into the side valley of Munstigeral. The valley cuts through the lower slopes of fan-shaped rock debris left by the retreating glacier hundreds of years ago. Keep to your left of the river (which will be the true right bank) and walk uphill by road to the upper level of the village.

□ About 100yd (91m) beyond the village, the road, which by now is becoming a cart track, forks. Take the left fork and climb a zigzag route, at first through alpine meadows and then through forest. This is the Gommer Höhenweg, the long distance path which follows the upper valley from Oberwald to Bellwald. The waymarking is a white-red-white block.

□ At a junction of paths, still inside the forest, turn left on a level track as far as a group of farm buildings at Tomebine.

There will be glimpses of the Goms valley and its surrounding peaks across clearings in the forest, and below of the open fields close to the farm at Tomebine.
The farm buildings are only used in summer when cattle are taken high above the main valley farms, to graze on the lush alpine herbiage.

□ Turn left at Tomebine and walk through delightful meadowland in front of the farms. The path swings to the right above Reckingen and aims towards the upper limits of the village.

□ Walk through the village to Reckingen station or the car park.

Reckingen's baroque church, built in the eighteenth century, is thought to be one of the finest in the area. Tragedy struck this village one night a decade or so ago, when an avalanche swept down from the Galmihorn Glacier burying a great number of the houses on the east side of the village. Worst hit was the barracks filled with soldiers, who were billeted there during their annual territorial service.

$7\frac{1}{2}$ miles (12km), 3-$3\frac{1}{2}$ hours. Easy.

This is valley walking at its best; an easily-followed path winds its way through lush pasture with shady forest never too far away. There is little or no climbing along the level track which follows the river, here almost straight as an arrow, but still full of the turbulence of its birth high up on the end of the complex tongues of the Rhône Glacier.

Evenly-spaced villages (one almost suspects that the canny Swiss planned it so) offer refreshment of all kinds at friendly gasthofs and cafés in their streets and tiny squares.

The walk is easy to follow; it starts by Oberwald station and follows the true left bank of the river downstream to Münster. The only time that it may be necessary to change sides is to visit one or other of the intervening villages for a lunch break or other refreshment stop.

The Route

□ Turn right outside Oberwald station and walk through the village. If it is preferred, and you have arrived by car, it will be necessary to return to Oberwald by a later train from Münster.

Notice the stone avalanche screen protecting the tiny village church in Oberwald.

□ Walk very slightly uphill towards the forest which can be seen ahead, across a short stretch of meadow, but do not enter the forest. Turn right along its lower edge on a footpath which will be signposted to Obergesteln. Walk downhill with the meadow on the right and the limits of the forest on your left hand. The path is simplicity itself, gradually working its way towards and then along the left bank of the river, downstream, through alpine pasture.

□ After walking for about 2 miles (3.2km) from Oberwald and where the path comes closest to the river, a bridge on the right can be crossed if you wish to visit Obergesteln.

Refreshments are available on the far side of Obergesteln village, on or near the main road.

□ From the Obergesteln turn-off, a farm road climbs away from the river and skirts the lower edge of the forested slopes of the main valley before turning towards a side valley, the Agene. Turn right on the valley road and follow it for about ½ mile (800m), towards Ulrichen.

Do not cross the river unless you wish to visit the village.

The minor road which you join in the Agene valley is the Nufenenpass road. It connects the Obergoms valley with the Bedretta and the Leventina valleys in the Italian-speaking Ticino canton of southern Switzerland.

□ About 100yd (91m) on the Nufenenpass side of the river, a cart track turns downstream, away from the road. Follow this past a group of farm buildings and into the riverside meadows of Hinnermatt. Follow the river for about 2½ miles (4km), ignoring the bridge and turning for Geschinen unless you wish to visit the village. The track continues through meadows scented with freshly-cut hay, or coloured with the spectrum of alpine flowers depending on the time of year and the weather. Deep pine forests clothe the steep valley sides and occasional glimpses show peaks and crags towering high above the path. Towards Münster the track passes through stretches of sparse woodland, where the shade can provide welcome relief on a hot summer's day.

□ Where another track joins from the left, turn right and cross the river and the railway, then left alongside the railway track as far as Münster station. Follow the station road uphill and into the village with its choice of restaurants and hotels.

Oberwald

5 miles (8km), 5 hours. Moderate/strenuous. Steep ascent at first.

The steep climb of about one mile (1.6km) through the Bawald forest in the early stages of this walk is amply rewarded by views framed between pines, or beyond forest clearings. Across the main valley, snow-capped peaks and rocky ridges tower above the eastern slopes. To the right, the Rhône Glacier will be seen as a frozen cascade beneath the towering arms of the Galenstock and the Gelmerhörner. Directly opposite as you climb, is the crest of the Aargrat ridge with the Sidelhorn — 9,069ft (2,764m), a comparative pimple on its northern end. This peak is a possible climb for ambitious walkers on another day, providing they are experienced in hill walking.

Oberwalderblasen is the steep hillside to the south-east, above the treeline. This is where local farmers still take cattle for summer grazing once the snow has cleared.

The walk starts from Oberwald station and finishes at Ulrichen. Motorists are therefore recommended to park at Ulrichen and take the train as far as Oberwald.

The Route

□ Leave Oberwald station by turning to the right, and walk to the far end of the village.

□ Where the village street turns left, leave it by turning right onto a footpath, signposted to Obergesteln. Keep left at a fork about 100yd (91m) uphill and climb steeply through the pine forest for about one mile (1.6km).

□ Bear right at a fork on the upper edge of the forest and climb, still by a zigzag path, out onto the open hillside.

□ After about ½ mile (800m) of steep climbing, a footpath junction is reached. Take the left fork. The angle of ascent eases a little and follows a contouring route at first to the left, then to the right, around the spur of the hillside.

□ Pass a group of mountain barns at Blasestafel and climb, more easily now, across the Oberwalderblasen to follow a tiny stream almost to the highest point of the hill.

Spend plenty of time crossing the Oberwalderblasen. The name, incidentally, means 'the breezy place above the forest'. Alpine flowers beneath your feet will compete with the views of the Rhône Glacier and the Aargrat ridge on the opposite side of the valley.

☐ Follow the path downhill, eventually walking by the side of a drainage channel which is followed into the forest beyond the old farm buildings at Randstafel.

☐ Walk steeply downhill through pine forest for about 1¼ miles (2km) ignoring the side paths to the left or right. Cross an open section and turn right, back into the forest at a footpath junction.

☐ On reaching open ground below the forest edge, follow a zigzag track through meadows beyond a group of farm buildings. Walk down into the Agene valley.

☐ On reaching the Nufenenpass road, do not follow it, but cross over and cut downhill between the massive zigzag bends needed to help road vehicles climb this steep hillside. Cross the road a second time and join it again lower down to reach the hamlet of Zum Loch.

☐ Continue by road through Zum Loch then across the river to reach Ulrichen station and the end of the walk. Refreshments will be available in the village which is about 250yd (229m) further on.

The Rhône Glacier

7½ miles (12km), 6-8 hours. Strenuous — 4,029ft (1,228m) steep ascent.

This is unquestionably a tough, steep climb, but one where the effort involved in the climb is amply rewarded. A carefully-engineered path climbs the steep hillside in a series of zigzags, which take a lot of the effort out of the angle of the slope. The view on reaching the Trützisee (the Trout Lake), makes the struggle worthwhile. This is a true alpine setting; steep rocky hillsides climb to snow-covered ridges and the turquoise lake is the jewel in the centre of this majestic alpine crown.

The peaks of the Mittaghorn (9,892ft, 3,015m) and the Brudelhorn (9,154ft, 2,790m), can be seen across the main valley, guarding either side of the 8,130ft (2,478m) Nufenen Pass which carries one of the highest motor roads in the Alps.

The walk starts and finishes in Geschinen (nearest railway station — Münster). On the outward leg the path follows the south-western ridge above the Geschinerbach stream and on the return crosses the north-eastern ridge.

The Route

□ Leave the centre of Geschinen village by following the Gommer Höhenweg white-red-white waymarking, to the right away from the houses, in the direction of the Geschinerbach stream.

□ Turn left at a junction of paths a little way above the stream. Still follow the white-red-white symbols and climb into the sparse pine forest.

□ At a footpath junction beyond point 1533, which should be signposted to Trützisee, turn right. Climb uphill on broad zigzags through the intermittent copses of the Birchwald.

The hillside gradually changes from patches of high alpine pasture surrounded by sparse woodland, to steeper rockier ground, the haunt of chamois and marmots. Alpine flowers in abundance, especially alpen rose, clothe the sheltered sunny slopes and birdlife is almost tame.

Pause for breath once you have cleared the trees and admire the views across the valley.

☐ Keep to the right of the ridge and ignore any side paths. The hillside steepens above the treeline, but the cleverly-designed path uses the easiest ground.

☐ Below point 2364, the path swings to the right below the ridge follows an easier course across the rock-strewn hillside.

Even though the angle of ascent has eased there is still a more than 750ft (228m) ascent before the Trützisee is reached! Pause frequently at this altitude and admire the magnificent scenery.

☐ At a junction with a path coming from the far side of the valley, turn left and climb the last steep part of the walk. Pass an ancient hut and follow the outlet stream all the way up to the lake.

Flagging spirits will soon revive on reaching the lake at the end of the steep climb from Geschinen. Trützisee makes an ideal picnic spot, but beware, as the lake water will be too cold for swimming! Directly above, narrow ridges climb in graceful sweeps to the summit of the Löffelhorn (10,155ft, 3,095m). The glacially-formed combe which holds this lake faces south-east, and as a result its southern side will be in shadow during the hottest part of the day, offering cooling conditions after a long hot climb.

☐ Leaving the lake, walk downhill by the same path alongside the outlet stream, past the old barn at Oberstafel, as far as the footpath junction.

☐ Turn left at the junction, ignoring the outward path. Zigzag downhill to join the main stream which by now has been joined by a number of tributaries.

☐ Cross the Geschinerbach stream to follow an irrigation channel on an easy course across the rocky hillside beneath the Geschinergale 7,756ft, (2,364m).

☐ On reaching the treeline again, another path joins from the left. Turn right and follow it downhill in broad zigzags through sparse woodland and across sheltered alpine meadows.

☐ The Gommer Höhenweg is joined about halfway between Geschinen and Ulrichen; both villages are visible, to the right and left along the valley road.

☐ Turn right along the Gommer Höhenweg to follow its white-red-white waymarkings past the high-level farms at Bärg. The path takes an easy route downhill through lush meadows all the way to Geschinen.

MÜNSTER TO BIEL BY THE GOMMER HÖHENWEG

---

5 miles (8km), 2½ hours. Moderate.

If in following the walks suggested in this guide, Trützisee was a recent climb, then this will be a pleasant way of relaxing the muscles tired after a long hard climb.

The path follows an easy route through woodland and forest and is enlivened by flower-filled meadows with constant views of high alpine scenery on either hand. It is also an ideal walk for a hot day.

The walk from Münster to Biel follows the white-red-white block waymarking of the Gommer Höhenweg — the Goms Highway. There are railway stations at both Münster and Biel which can be used either for the outward or return journeys if travelling by car.

The Route

□ If travelling by train, follow the station road into the centre of Münster. Cross the village square and take the narrow street which climbs a little way into the Münstigertal valley.

□ Cross the river by an old watermill on the right. Almost immediately the road joins a farm lane at a T junction. White-red-white block symbols indicate that this is the Gommer Höhenweg.

□ Turn left along the track and climb gently uphill across meadowland towards the edge of the pine-covered lower slopes of the Galmihorn (11,1438ft, 3,486m).

□ Keep left at the junction of four paths by the farmstead of Gifi.

□ Walk on, still skirting the forest edge, and cross a small stream.

□ Go through a narrow belt of pine trees then out on to the sparsely-wooded upper slopes of meadows above Reckingen.

□ To the right of the farms of Wiler, paths lead off in several directions from a complex staggered junction. Look out for the Gommer Höhenweg waymarks and fork right on a path contouring round the shoulder of the hill.

□ Go through an area of forest and cross the steep valley of the Reckingerbach.

The scoured nature of this side valley indicates the frequency with which avalanches sweep down from the Galmihorn in winter. Innocent in summer, the valley is a dangerous place in early spring when heavy snows begin to thaw. In summer the views across the main valley will make even the most amateurish photographer reach for a camera. Directly opposite, the Blinnenhorn (11,067ft, 3,373m), snow-capped throughout the year, towers majestically above its satellite peaks and ridges.

□ On the far side of the Reckingerbach valley, start to walk downhill into deep forest.

□ Above a clearing at the Bine farmsteads, the path forks; take the right-hand and climb slightly uphill leaving the forest for the rough ground of another winter avalanche zone.

Notice how nature has bowed to the depredations of frequent avalanches: the tallest trees clearly mark the boundary between safety and the danger zone. Alpine flowers such as coltsfoot and glacier crowfoot are quick to colonise ground which has been disturbed in winter. Plants such as the gentian need greater security and will be found further away from the avalanche path.

□ Climb into and then through forest on a broad path. Ignore the signposted path on the left to Ritzingen.

□ Cross the highest point of a steep alpine pasture and aim for the groups of farm buildings at Resti.

□ Turn left in front of the barns and walk on a steep downhill path into Biel, with forest to the right and flowery meadows on the left.

Biel has one or two cafés and the station is a little way below the village just above the main river.

The Furka Pass

6 THE GOMMER HÖHENWEG FROM MÜNSTER TO OBERWALD

6¼ miles (10km), 3 hours. Easy/moderate.

As Münster is the main and arguably the most interesting village in the Obergoms, it naturally claims our attention as the obvious starting or finishing point of a number of walks. Reached easily by train or road, or perhaps as a base for an enjoyable holiday in this area, it makes an ideal walking centre.

This walk is really an extension to the walk from Münster to Biel, and has been deliberately included as a means of dividing the Gommer Höhenweg into two comparatively easy day walks. The previous walk goes down the valley from Münster and this one, follows the valley upwards to make, it is hoped, an interesting comparison.

The route follows well-made footpaths which take the easiest gradients through meadows filled with flowers; and there are panoramic views of high alpine peaks across the valley. Diversions away from the main route can be made for refreshment at any of the conveniently-placed villages along the valley road.

The Route

□ Make your way to the right away from the centre of Münster, towards an area of open meadows on the north side of the village. Follow the Höhenweg white-red-white waymarks along the rough track which climbs through the meadows towards the farmsteads of Löümene.

An early start will show the field flowers at their best, and also give delightful views of the village of Münster and its unique baroque church silhouetted against the morning sun.

□ On reaching Löümene turn right, along a good footpath following the shoulder of the hillside towards a group of sparse pine trees and also rougher ground.

□ Ignore the Trützisee path on the left, but continue to walk ahead following the white-red-white block signs.

□ Follow the edge of slightly denser woodland downhill, towards, but not into Geschinen (unless an early refreshment stop is needed).

□ Beyond the Geschinen turning, continue to follow the Höhenweg signs, now uphill on a steeper track across the open hillside. Ignore paths off to the right or left until you reach a stream where the track forks.

□ Cross the stream and take the left fork to climb fairly steeply across the hillside above the village of Ulrichen, again ignoring paths on either side of the waymarked route.

□ Climb between two isolated sections of forest and cross the deep valley of the Oberbach. Beyond the stream the path follows an easier route, contouring across a steep hillside and between clumps of trees.

The view out of the Oberbach valley and across the main valley is of the lower reaches of the Nufenen Pass with the Mittaghorn (9,846ft, 3,001m) and Pic Gallina (10,040ft, 3,060m) dominating the left side of the pass, just 4½ miles (7¼km) away as the crow flies!

□ The path follows a steep downhill route to a group of farm buildings called Gadestatt. Below the barns the Höhenweg forks, one following a level track towards another farmstead group at Hostette. To the right of Gadestatt a narrow lane drops in an easy sweep to Obergesteln.

□ If you have been to Obergesteln for a refreshment stop, it will be necessary to rejoin the main path at Gadestatt. A lane waymarked with the white-red-white blocks follows an irrigation ditch away from the farmsteads, in a series of short zigzags towards the Milibach, one of the many feeders of the still infant Rhône.

□ Cross the Milibach and climb along the edge of a small wood to join the main path a little way beyond Hostette alp.

□ The path continues, now along an easy contouring route, in and out of forest, across the hillside before descending the short distance to Oberwald.

Oberwald and its near neighbour Unnerwasser have a wide choice of cafés and gasthofs and the valley train stops at Oberwald for the return journey.

7½ miles (12km), 4½-5 hours. Moderate/strenuous — 3,458ft (1,054m) descent.

The footpath from the top of the Furka Pass will excite the imagination of experienced walkers and first-time visitors alike. Starting at the summit of one of Europe's highest roads, the beautifully engineered footpath leads first across debris left by the retreating Mutt glacier; it then crosses a steep hillside where the views opposite are of the massive Rhône glacier. Finally the path drops by a series of careful zigzags into the Goms valley with Oberwald waiting to welcome and refresh tired walkers.

Many alpine flowers, some rare, will be seen on this route, especially in the upper reaches of the Lenges valley beneath the Tällistock peak. Gentians will colour some sections with their deep blues, whilst the yellow sulphur anemone can be found in grassy areas. The now rare edelweiss still flourishes on hidden ledges away from the depredations of uncaring plant collectors.

Check locally about train or postbus services to reach the nearest point to the Furkablick Hotel. Ideally you will need to travel by road to the hotel or reach the nearest point by rail, namely the Furka Halt by the north-eastern portal of the summit tunnel. A third alternative is to leave at the Muttabach Belvédère, but this will entail a climb of 1,027ft (313m) to reach the Furka summit.

The Route

□ The walk starts from the Furkablick Hotel at the summit of the Furka Pass (see note above for details of public transport).

The pass is the highest point of a fault which has left a huge cleft, dividing the Swiss Alps from Martigny to Chur; it has long been an important route between the Valais and Grisons cantons.

□ Leave the road by following the track signposted to Oberwald; it climbs in a southerly direction across the rocky lower slopes of the Blauberg ridge, itself a subsidiary of the Muttenhörner Massif — 10,168ft (3,099m).

□ Follow the path by carefully contouring beneath the glacial combe of the Mutten glacier.

The path crosses a boulder field left by the retreating glacier, which can be seen high up under the shapely peak of the Gross Muttenhorn.

□ Ignore a path which climbs to the left and over the minor Tällistock peak, but walk forwards by path, still on an easy contour across the rocky hillside of Hirsch-platten.

As you follow the contour round the shoulder above Hirsch-platten the view will be taking all of your attention. Directly opposite across the Mutt valley, the Rhône Glacier rises in terrifying ice waves to the eternal snows of the High Alps. The Galenstock – 11,756ft (3,583m) – encloses the eastern wall of the glacier and in the west the long ridge of the Gelmerhorner – 10,171ft (3,100m) – stretches in an almost straight line separating the Rhône Glacier from the Grimsel Pass.

□ Keep left away from the shoulder of the hill and walk downhill until the headwaters of the Lenges River are reached.

□ Follow the painted waymarks on prominent boulders, and pass isolated alpine barns dotted at intervals on the steep rocky slope.

At a footpath junction below the old farmstead of Gand the view opens up along the entire length of the Upper Goms valley.

□ Turn left at the junction below Gand and continue on this steep and rocky course as far as the treeline.

□ At a footpath junction beyond a large area of pine forest and at a footpath junction on the edge of a second pinewood, turn left and walk uphill, then round the shoulder of the mountain for about 500yd (550m) until the hill farms of Barg are reached.

□ Turn right away from the farms along their access track, downhill through alpine meadows to more farms at Gere.

□ From Gere a good road leads along the Goneri valley, improving as it descends to reach the village of Unterwasser and its neighbour Oberwald where the walk finishes.

The gorge of the lower Goneri makes a shady finish to the walk on a hot day.

THE SLOPES OF THE SIDELHORN FROM OBERGESTELN

8 miles (13km), 5 hours. Moderate.

A well-engineered footpath makes the climbing comparatively easy on this walk. There is a 2,500ft (762m) difference in height between Obergesteln in the valley bottom and the highest point reached on this walk, but the angle of ascent is never too steep. A series of zigzags, both uphill and down, make the effort of climbing the hillside so much less.

The path was built years ago to provide access to the high pastures used every summer by farmers whose main holdings are in and around villages lining the valley bottom. Cattle, sheep and goats are likely to be met near the summer farmsteads in the Chietal valley or at Sattelti. The animals take advantage of the lush pasture which follows the melting snow's retreat up the hillside. Milk is mostly converted into butter and cheese for later dispatch to central marketing organisations.

Flowers fill every space across this hillside and the walker will, no doubt, spend a happy hour or two walking in the high alpine meadows, where the views across the Upper Goms valley consist of the snowclad peaks surrounding the Mittaghorn.

The Route

□ Leave Obergesteln by the Münster road and after walking for a little over ¼ mile (402m) turn right, away from the road, along a cart track which will be marked with the Höhenweg white-red-white symbol.

□ Climb the grassy hillside as far as the farms of Wiler. Turn right in front of the farm buildings and walk on a gentler gradient to the Gadestatt farmsteads.

The path so far is through typical alpine meadowland with its profusion of flowery growth which lasts until haymaking time.

□ Turn left through the Gadestatt settlement as far as the corner of a small pine wood.

□ Turn right at the pine wood, away from the Höhenweg, to follow a narrower path climbing in broad sweeps up the tree-scattered hillside.

□ The path enters the top level of a pine forest, and then swings back to the right out onto the open hillside.

As you climb higher, the lush grazing of the lower slopes gives way to sparser grasses and smaller ground-hugging plant life. This is the zone where the rarer alpine flowers will usually be found.

□ Gradually the angle of ascent eases until at about point 2167, where the track swings to the right around the shoulder of the hill and enters the Chietal valley.

□ Cross a rocky stream bed.

Shade provided by rocks on either side of the Milibach stream in Chietal makes this an ideal picnic spot.

□ Climb the swelling curve of the hillside above the Chietal valley as far as the ancient farmsteads of Bodme.

□ Begin to walk downhill and cross an area of irrigation ditches carrying water from the Jost stream to farms lower down the hillside. Cross the stream itself.

□ Turn right at a junction with a wider path coming down the hillside from the Grimselpass.

It is possible to alter the walk at this point by turning left to climb to the Grimselpass where the Totesee, the Lake of the Dead, commemorates the nearby battle between the Austrians and French in 1799. If using this alternative, a well-marked path crosses the rocky eastern slopes of the Sidelhorn to reach the lake. There is a comfortable hotel and restaurant on the summit of the Grimselpass. Follow the road for a little way downhill, and avoid its sharp bends by using the path to Gletsch and the railway station.

□ To follow the main route back to Obergesteln, use the Grimselpass path downhill away from the junction as mentioned above to Sattelti.

□ The path swings to the left and right across an open hillside, which gradually improves as outcropping rocks are abandoned in favour of alpine pasture and pine forest.

□ On the forest edge, walk ahead at a path junction.

□ Swing left between two clearings and zigzag downhill beneath shade of mature pines.

□ Cross the railway and turn right to reach Oberwald.

CHAMPEX

Maps

Landeskarte der Schweiz (1:50,000 series) Sheet 5003 — Mont Blanc — Grand Combin; or Sheet 282 — Martigny.

How to get there:

Road:

South by European motorway system via Basel and Bern to Montreux

South-east to Martigny, then by the Grand Saint Bernard Pass to Orsières. A steep side road climbs to Champex in a series of zigzags.

Rail:

Main line services to Geneva and Martigny. Branch line to Orsières followed by postbus.

Air:

International airport at Geneva, connection by rail and postbus.

The Area

Often ignored by tourists who may be more interested in reaching the honeypot at the Hospice of Saint Bernard, Champex is hidden away in a fold of the mountains above the main valley of the Drance. Reached only by a steep zigzag road from Orsières, the mountain resort can offer much to the holidaymaker who wants peaceful surroundings, mountain air, forest, a quiet lake, and above all, magnificent alpine scenery close at hand.

Napoleon came this way during his campaign against the Austrians at the time of the Battle of Marengo, a battle commemorated by a chicken dish invented by his overworked chef, who made the most of a rather poor quality chicken.

Champex is part of the Valais region of Switzerland, and the cuisine has a definite French flavour. Cheese fondues are a speciality hereabouts and trout, abundant in local lakes and streams, are cooked to carefully guarded recipes. Wines come from the local vineyards of the upper Rhône, with Dôle, a delicate red, the favourite.

This countryside is steeped in tradition. On festival days, local women wear distinctive dresses and hats made from over fifty yards of ruched silk. Special dances, often held outdoors to the music of fiddles, are organised, especially in August, the time of the main festival.

Walking can be as varied as anyone could want, from a high-level tour to visit the Trient glacier or a valley walk down to Sembrancher in the main valley. There are many easy local walks around the village of Champex, either by a simple tour of its lake or an easy climb to the *Jardin Alpin Florealpe,* a fine collection of alpine plants in their natural setting. Champex is surrounded by pine forests cloaking the lower slopes of nearby mountains. Well-marked tracks through these forests can be used on hot days, when open hillsides can feel almost like an oven.

Refreshment on the walks should be no problem, as most of the surrounding hamlets have some sort of café. Some farms will be able to offer a drink, even if it is only fresh milk, which always manages to taste better in the mountains than the bottled variety town-dwellers are accustomed to drinking.

Entertainment is very much a low-key affair. There is no high life with nightclubs and casinos; but if an informal, quiet, friendly dance, or a local concert is more your idea of what a mountain resort should offer then Champex is the place to visit. There is a swimming pool, and boating on the lake. The chair lift to la Breya can be used either for a lazy sunny afternoon, or as the start of an easy scramble along the ridge.

Useful Information

Local Tourist Office
Office du Tourisme
CH — 1938 Champex
Telephone: 026 4 12 27

Accommodation
High-class hotels, apartments, dormitories, youth hostels and campsites.

Chair Lift
Télésiège Breya (chair, 2 stages)

Glacier Viewing
Glacier flights by light aircraft, available from Sociéte Air — Glacier, l'Areodrome de Sion.

From Chamonix the following Mont Blanc Glaciers are easily accessible: Mer de Glas (by train from Chamonix), Glacier des Bossons (immediately above the Mt. Blanc tunnel), Glacier d'Argentière (by cable car from Argentière).

St Bernard Hospice and Pass
Take the old road via Orsières to the top of the St Bernard Pass.

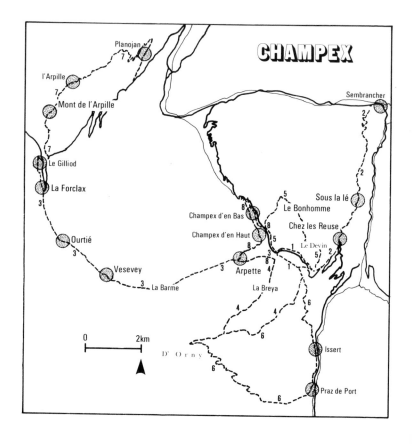

---

3 miles (4.8km), $1\frac{1}{2}$-2 hours. Easy.

This is a popular Sunday afternoon or summer evening walk; an ideal first day's excursion after a long journey. It also helps the visitor to explore the village and possibly plan further walks through the surrounding forests and across nearby hillsides.

Two other features are highlighted on this walk. The first and most obvious is the lake, set in its mountain hollow and surrounded by flower-bedecked chalets. The second, which only reveals itself as the walker arrives at its gates, is the alpine garden. The *Jardin Florealpe* is in a natural setting amongst the rocks on the hillside above the village. Here 4,000 different specimens of flowers from all over the alps are displayed, and help the visitor to understand their individual environmental requirements.

The walk follows the easiest of footpaths around the lake, then on through meadows towards a quiet river. Crossing this, the route climbs a little way to the alpine garden, before following a balcony path back to the village, which is rarely out of sight throughout the walk.

The Route

☐ The walk starts at the eastern end of lac de Champex. Take the track from between the boat hire and the Taverne Pilon restaurant and walk past the Hotel d'Orny towards the Catholic church.

☐ Turn right beyond the church and walk towards the lake. Cross its outflow and follow the shoreline to the left as far as the Protestant chapel.

☐ Fork left on to the *chemin du Revers* path and walk through mature larch and pine forest towards the river on the far side of a slight rise. Go under a ski-lift cable which follows a man-made break in the forest.

☐ Turn right and cross the river by the bridge. Walk past a barn with marshy meadowland on its right.

☐ Join the metalled road and walk towards a right-angled bend opposite les Arollas.

☐ Turn left away from the road to follow a track past the campsite and skirting the edge of dense mature pine forest. The path, the *Tour de Champex,* swings round to the right and continues in this direction beyond a junction with another path.

□ Follow the gently rising path through woodland to the alpine garden.

The Jardin Alpin Florealpe has been carefully built up with plants collected in the Swiss Alps and other mountain areas.

□ Start to walk downhill, back towards the upper buildings of Champex, and reach the lakeside road by turning right at a junction with a track below the Hotel Splendide. The track joins the road opposite the boat hire cabin.

Champex

5½ miles (9km), 3½ hours. Easy/moderate.

The walk follows a gradually descending route, through forest and across sunny alpine pastures high above the Drance Valley, to reach the busy little town of Sembrancher.

Traffic seen far below on the road from Sembrancher to Orsières will be heading towards the Grand St Bernard Pass, and although tourists will probably use the old road over the pass, commercial vehicles and others will go under the pass route by the tunnel, which is open all the year, into Northen Italy. The St Bernard route was taken by Napoleon on his way to fight the Austrians at the Battle of Marengo. He stayed overnight at an hotel in Orsières but left early the next day without paying his bill. The bill is now a proud possession of the present hotelier. The famous St Bernard Hospice still stands on the summit of the pass, but fortunately the monks and their dogs are no longer required to rescue travellers battling their way across the pass on foot through winter snows.

A series of high-level farming communities are visited on the way to Sembrancher; it is worth spending a little time in each hamlet exploring its hidden corners and getting to know the interesting people who live on these sunny alps.

The Route

□ Turn left away from the eastern end of the lake and walk along the road between the boutique and the Café de la Promenade. Pass the Belvédère Hotel and walk as far as the Alpine Restaurant car park.

□ Take the first path on the left at the side of the Alpine and walk straight on, gradually downhill, through dense pine forest as far as point 1330 at a bend on the winding Champex-Orsières road.

□ Turn left, downhill, away from the road to walk along the upper edge of the steep sided open hillside as far as a second hairpin bend in the road.

□ The path, skirting the bend, climbs craggy forested slopes above the farm settlement of Chez les Reuse.

There is a worthwhile diversion to the right through Chez les Reuse, turn left along a track on the far side of the settlement to regain the main route.

□ Follow the upper edge of the Chez les Reuse clearing. Go through a narrow belt of forest and cross a narrow ravine by a well-made track.

□ Beyond the ravine, fork right on the main track, across open meadows above Verlona.

□ Walk through Verlona and two woodland belts to reach a high-level road to the scattered settlement of Sous la Lé.

□ Follow a gently winding track through meadows and between clumps of pine and larch. Cross a small stream, beyond which the track cuts across the steepening hillside to reach La Garde.

□ Keep left through La Garde, eventually walking down a dry valley.

□ Bear left around a wooded knoll.

□ Join a jeep track and turn left.

□ Follow the track downhill along its zigzag route as far as Sembrancher station.

After exploring Sembrancher – it has a good selection of shops and restaurants – return to Champex by train to Orsières and then connecting postbus or taxi, to avoid the steep 1,854ft (565m) climb back to up the hill.

Family hiking in Switzerland

---

10 miles (16km), 5-6 hours. Strenuous — 3,935ft (1,199m).

Providing the Fenêtre d'Arpette is free of snow, this is an exciting high-level walk which will take you into a tiny corner of the complex of peaks and glaciers surrounding the Mont Blanc massif. From the top of the pass there opens an awe-inspiring view directly across the upper Trient valley, to the jagged ice falls and deep crevasses of the Glacier du Trient. On a hot day rumblings from deep within the glacier or the tearing crash of falling blocks of ice act as a reminder that glaciers are not stationary features, but rivers of ice, constantly on the move however slowly this may be.

The route followed by this walk is one of the optional diversionary sections of the Tour of Mont Blanc. Waymarking TMB signs indicate the route of this long-distance footpath from Chamonix round the highest mountain in Europe. It follows well-marked paths across easy passes from France into Switzerland and back by way of Italy and the upper Aosta valley. The walk is safe, simple to follow and yet never strays far from some of the most dramatic mountain scenery in the world.

Two valleys are used on the walk described here; the first, Val d'Arpette, is uphill and has the easier gradient. The way down into the Trient valley from the top of the Fenêtre d'Arpette pass is over steeper terrain; however the path is well-made and easy to follow.

The walk finishes on the other side of the mountains, well away from Champex, so check the times of transport back from Trient by way of Martigny before setting out.

The Route

□ Leave Champex by following the road and track as far as the Breya chair lift's lower station.

□ Turn right beneath the lift to follow a woodland path aross the lower slopes of la Breya mountain.

□ Join the river and follow it upstream past mountain farms and outlying barns at Arpette.

□ Continue to walk upstream over grazing areas which gradually give way to rockier ground.

□ Still alongside the river, cross from one side, then the other, as dictated by the waymarked path.

□ Leave the treeline behind and begin to climb over rocky ground to the remote La Barme alp.

□ Fork right beneath a rocky outcrop and climb steeply through a series of tiered crags.

The lower scree-covered slopes are the remains of a small glacier which disappeared in the late 1800s.

□ Follow the waymarks up the final steep scree and boulder covered slopes to the Fenêtre d'Arpette (literally, the window of Arpette).

The view from the pass is worth all the effort involved in the climb. Opposite is the Trient glacier sweeping down in a frozen cascade from the Aiguille du Tour – 11,618ft (3,540m). The mountain is away on the left, better viewed from the path lower down the valley. Beyond the Aiguille rise the peaks and ridges of the fantastic mountain region – the Mont Blanc massif.

□ Walk down the steep path into the Trient valley. Turn left beneath a series of massive crags to reach the remote summer farm of Vesevey.

□ Zigzag down through boulderfields and glacier-worn slabs and rocks as far as the treeline.

□ Go left, down past the Ourtié farm to the river. (Ignore a path alongside an irrigation ditch on the right, away from the river).

□ Cross the river and turn right to climb above its ravine.

□ Follow the rocky woodland path high above the river until it drops down to more open and level ground, close to l'Odéyi farmstead.

□ Walk down the widening valley, across the Nant Noir side stream and through a narrow but pretty pine wood.

□ Cross meadowland to reach le Peuty, an outlying settlement of Trient.

□ Follow the lane into Trient.

□ Return by postbus over the Forclaz pass to Martigny and from there to Champex either by train to Orsières or by the more direct postbus.

---

4

8 miles (12.9km), 4-5 hours. Moderate.

Aided by the Breya chair lift this high-level walk takes the visitor safely into realms normally only open to the mountaineer. The chair lift saves something in the nature of 2,260ft (689m) of climbing to the summit of la Breya — 7,181ft (2,188m). Beyond it, more than half of the length of the walk is spent around the 2,000m contour line.

The path beyond la Breya skirts the razor-sharp edge of a rocky ridge before descending beneath the Col de la Breya into the wild Combe d'Orny. On reaching the torrent of the Darbellay river, the hillwalker is faced with the decision either to follow the river downstream, or turn right and climb about 656ft (200m) through the slabs of the combe to the d'Orny hut. This hut lies near a small glacial lake at the foot of the d'Orny glacier, a side outflowing of the Trient, that massive snow and ice field below the Aiguille du Tour — 11,618ft (3,540m). Following the valley below Combe d'Orny is a straightforward affair and afterwards a side path leads away through pine forest to the Prassurny col below Champex.

The Route

□ Take the chair lift from the western end of Champex village to the summit of la Breya.

The rocky terrace outside the top station is an excellent viewpoint for the surrounding peaks as well as the valley of the Drance, far below and to the east of la Breya. Lake Champex looks like a turquoise jewel from this height.

□ Follow the path signposted to Combe d'Orny away from the chair lift towards higher ground, but unless you are qualified to climb the tricky ridge, keep to the well-made and waymarked path below its crest.

□ Walk beneath the shattered ridge on a level path which keeps to the contour-line.

□ Climb gradually beyond the final outcropping needle aiming towards the Col de la Breya.

□ Join a path crossing the col from Val d'Arpette and turn left.

□ Follow the rocky path across a scree slope, beneath supporting lower crags of the pinnacles of the Aiguilles d'Arpette.

□ Follow a roughly contouring path into the valley and as far as its river.

□ If time and energy permit, turn right at the junction with this valley path and climb across a series of glacier worn 'boiler plate' rocks (they are rounded and look like whale backs) as far as the Swiss Alpine Club's Cabine d'Orny. (Refreshments are available here.)

Beyond the hut and set in a wilderness of glacial rubble is a tiny emerald-green lake. Its parent, the d'Orny glacier, is at this level a dirty rock-strewn mess, but higher up it becomes white.

□ Continue down the valley (or turn left here if you have not been to the hut).

□ Climb over ice-worn outcropping rocks and slabs downhill following a zigzag route, keeping away from the deep ravine of the middle river.

□ Swing left, beneath the crags, on a grass-covered slope to reach the river.

□ Cross the river and follow it downstream along its left bank to the upper limits of the treeline.

□ At a junction of paths fork left, away from the river, into pine forest.

□ Follow the roughly contouring path around the shoulder of one of la Breya's buttresses and then walk easily downhill.

□ Walk over a footpath crossing at point 1500.

□ Leave the forest to cross an open avalanche zone. The gash is made by late winter snows but is safe in summer.

□ Walk down to the more level slopes above Prassurny and follow the path to the left and back to Champex.

LE BONHOMME

5

(7,991ft, 2,435m)

7½ miles (12km), 6 hours. Moderate/strenuous — 3,177ft (968m) ascent.

This is a stiff climb; the angle of ascent hardly varies, all the way from Champex to the top of Le Bonhomme. However on reaching the summit of this good natured mountain (as its name implies), the climber is rewarded by unforgettable views of the surrounding peaks. All eyes will, of course, turn to the west at first, and scan the huge mass of dramatic peaks and glaciers overtopped by the snow-covered dome of Mont Blanc. That is not all; to the south-east lies the rock and ice barrier which marks the border between Switzerland and Italy. The stately needle of the Matterhorn is easy to pick out on a clear day, and backing it is the bulk of Monte Rosa.

This natural barrier divides the peoples of Europe into two distinct groups; to the north of the mountain range they are of central European origin, yet only a few miles away across the ridge in Italy, the people are clearly Mediterranean.

Climbing above Champex, the footpath follows a forested route, first to one side and then the other on the southern ridge of Le Bonhomme, to reach the summit rocks above the treeline. A reasonably level track traverses beneath the connecting ridge of the Points des Chevrettes to meet Le Catogne — 8,527ft (2,598m) path in a combe below the summit of the latter. Downwards and back into the forest, the route leads directly to the valley road close by Champex d'en Haut.

The Route

☐ Follow the Orsières track out of Champex to the east of the village as far as the Alpina restaurant.

☐ Turn left in front of the restaurant to follow a signposted footpath, the Chemin du Devin.

☐ Climb steeply uphill on a slanting path through forest, beneath the rocky ridge.

☐ In the area of forest known as le Devin, swing left and climb across the ridge by a zigzag route, following white-red-white waymarks.

☐ On the far side of the ridge, the angle eases and the path follows a level course for a short way.

Tree-framed views of the peaks beyond Val d'Arpette and la Breya are seen through gaps in the forest.

□ At point 1794 join a steep path from Champex above a rocky outcrop. Turn right and zigzag uphill on increasingly rocky ground.

□ Beyond the treeline the path joins the south ridge; follow it all the way to the top of Le Bonhomme.

Le Bonhomme is an excellent vantage point for the peaks of the Valais and also the Mont Blanc massif.

□ Continue beyond the summit rocks, north-west along a gently-descending path beneath the ridge.

Constant views of the Mont Blanc massif.

□ Turn left at a footpath junction and descend steeply along the edge of the pine forest.

□ Enter the forest to walk down a steep rocky gully.

Take extra care on this section as the rock is often loose.

□ The path crosses avalanche clearings, but keeps mostly to the shade of the forested slopes until it reaches the road.

□ Join the road and turn left opposite the farm settlement of Champex d'en Haut. Follow the quiet road all the way back to Champex.

COMBE D'ORNY AND THE CHEVRETTES RIDGE

---

6

11 miles (17.7km), 8 hours. Strenuous — 2,905ft (885m) ascent.

Try to make an early start for this walk. Much of the route, especially over its upper rocky sections, is exposed to the full strength of the sun. Unless the wise precaution of wearing a wide-brimmed hat and a long-sleeved shirt is taken, the sun's rays can cause severe burning to exposed arms and neck. Sunburn on the back of the neck is particularly dangerous as it can lead to sunstroke; barrier creams are helpful, but the safest practice in strong sunlight is to keep covered up. Sunglasses are another essential.

Climbing out of the Prassurny forest, the path turns the broad eastern shoulder of La Breya to climb beyond the treeline to the glacier-worn slabs and debris of Combe d'Orny. Reaching the shelter of the Cabine d'Orny brings a welcome rest before the descent across a gap in the Chevrettes ridge. The final part of the high-level section is a steep descent to the Saleina valley where a woodland route leads back through Val Ferret to Champex.

The hard climb to up the Combe d'Orny can be simplified by using the Breya chair lift and following the route described in the fourth walk in this section to the d'Orny hut. From Praz de Fort, the postbus via Orsières will cut short the climb from the Drance valley, but if energies and time allow, this final attractive woodland ramble is a highly recommended finish to a memorable mountain walk.

Even if you do not at the outset intend using the postbus from Praz de Fort, it would be a wise precaution to check the schedule beforehand.

The Route

□ Walk around the western end of Lake Champex, past the Protestant chapel and across the woodland clearing.

□ On the edge of the next area of forest, take a right-hand path, signposted to Combe d'Orny. Follow the white-red-white block waymarkings through the pinewood, as the track goes gently uphill and around the shoulder of la Breya.

□ Follow the path steadily uphill, through a rocky clearing, formed by avalanches, as far as a footpath crossing.

□ Walk on at the crossing and contour to the left, beneath scree slopes, into Combe d'Orny.

□ Walk down to the river, turn right and follow it steeply upstream.

□ Cross the stream at point 1640 and work away from it on the zigzag path.

□ Climb through an area of scree and then on to glacier-worn slabs.

□ Return to the river, cross over and walk up to the d'Orny hut. (Refreshments available).

□ Walk a little way uphill, away from the hut and beyond the glacier lake.

□ Turn left on the signposted path across the terminal moraines of the d'Orny glacier, walk downhill to a col in the Chevrettes ridge.

□ Continue downhill — the path is steeper now — on a zigzag track, gradually leaving the scree-littered ridge for the broadening lower valley of the Saleina river.

The main valley into which the Reuse de Saleina flows is Val Ferret, which leads to an easy road-free col into Italy. On the right and entering the Saleina valley is the narrow final stage of the Glacier de Saleina.

□ Follow the path as far as Praz de Fort (refreshments and shops). The postbus calls at this village and could be used to cut short the walk.

□ Walk down the quiet valley road to Issert village and beyond it to point 1049.

□ Turn left, away from the road to follow footpaths waymarked TMB (Tour of Mont Blanc).

□ Climb through the shady forest to point 1211. Turn right over the Jureau stream, then after 650yd (600m) cross the swift-flowing Darbella, the same stream which was followed earlier along Combe d'Orny. Follow the forest path, gradually uphill, until it reaches a wide bend in the Orsières/Champex road.

□ Turn left gently uphill, along the road to reach Champex.

---

5 miles (8km), 2½ hours. Easy.

The middle Rhône valley, being sheltered from maritime winds by the highest mountain masses in Europe, is the driest and sunniest part of Switzerland; south-facing slopes are covered with vineyards soaking up this Mediterranean style climate. To reach the start of the walk it will be necessary to drive beneath vineyards along the Martigny/Forclaz road to a point below the hill village of Ravoire, where an access road leaves the main highway at la Fontaine. Leave the car at this point and catch the Martigny/Forclaz postbus to the bottom station of the Arpille chair lift at Forclaz. Check the timetable beforehand.

Postbuses serve most of the out-of-the-way places in Switzerland, and run to reliable timetables. Travelling on them is an easy and cheap way to get the feel of local life, and the character of the villages along the bus route. Concessionary runabout tickets make travelling by bus very reasonable.

The Route

□ Either take the postbus or drive from Champex to Martigny. Follow the Forclaz Pass road through la Croix, and climb by motorised transport through vineyards filling the nearby slope.

□ Leave the car at the Ravoire turning (point 911 on the Landeskarte der Schweiz map, Sheet No 282— Martigny). Catch the postbus to la Forclaz.

□ Take the chair lift to the top of the treeline on Mont de l'Arpille.

There is a marvellous panoramic view from the top station; it covers the north (French) face of Mont Blanc with the spire of the Aiguille du Midi towering above Chamonix. To the left lie the huge Valais mountains of the Monte Rosa group, including the Matterhorn.

□ Walk on from the upper station over the flower-filled Arpille plateau to its highest point — 6,843ft (2,085m).

□ Follow the broad, easy, northern ridge until it begins to descend steeply.

□ Turn right following the well defined path which carefully avoids the steepest part of the ridge.

□ Walk down to the l'Arpille high-level summer farm settlement. *Spend a little time looking at the old timber buildings of l'Arpille, but do not disturb the people whose home is on this lovely alp.*

□ Walk through the settlement and across its meadows towards the upper edge of larch woodland, keeping slightly to the right to reach the treeline.

□ Follow the woodland edge until a footpath makes itself apparent. Follow this through the forest all the way down to Ravoire.

□ Catch the postbus back to the main road.

Grapes grown on the vineyard below Ravoire are used for Valais wines. Not well known outside this region, the wines are nevertheless of a high quality, ranging from the white Fendant, and also Johannisberg which has a delicate Rhine wine bouquet, to Dôle, the most popular Swiss red; this is a fragrant, full-bodied wine, a blend of black pinot and gamay grapes.

The look-out terrace of La Breya (see Walk 4)

5 miles (8km), 2-3 hours. Easy.

Here is an opportunity to have an easier walk; perhaps it may be used to follow several harder days spent on steeper ground and tougher walks, or perhaps just an easy day is required. This walk is also suitable for filling in a morning or afternoon when the rest of the day is taken up by other plans.

The series of paths and forest tracks followed by this walk wander through dense larch and pine forest of the lower Val d'Arpette, to remote and unspoilt farming communities. Time seems to have stood still in these little settlements and the few people you meet will be more than happy to pass the time of day. Their local French dialect may be beyond the linguistic ability of many; though with a little patience and a few smiles, communication becomes easier.

The Route

□ The walk starts from the eastern end of lac de Champex. Turn right away from the road, walk down the lane at the back of the landing stage, towards the Catholic church.

□ Turn right beyond the church and walk down to the lake shore. Follow this route, through woodland, as far as the footpath junction near the Protestant chapel.

The village of Champex looks at its most attractive when viewed through pine boughs on the shoreline.

□ Fork left at the junction to follow the path along the lower edge of the forest and above the swampy riverside meadows. Walk under the ski tow cable.

□ On reaching the river, turn right over the bridge and then left through a small meadow. Turn left along the lane to reach the bottom stage of the Breya chair lift, recrossing the river on the way.

□ Turn right beneath the chair lift cable and walk steadily uphill along a winding forest track.

On a hot day the shade offered by the forest will be most welcome. Distant views open beyond the forest clearings.

□ The path, which still climbs gradually inside the forest, turns the shoulder of the lower slopes of la Breya to enter the steep-sided narrow middle section of Val d'Arpette.

Ignore a path on the left coming down from the summit of la Breya.

▢ The angle of the path eases and on reaching the river, skirts the edge of the clearing of the Arpette meadows.

If you are fortunate enough to reach Arpette before haymaking time, the views across its flowery meadows will be quite breathtaking. Even after haymaking, it can still be a wonderful sight with distant forests making a frame around the view of the rocky peaks. To the left, looking along the valley, the eye will be drawn to the ridges on either side of the pass of the Fenêtre d' Arpette, the climax of the third walk in this section.

▢ Follow the forest path, which goes downhill, gradually becoming steeper as it follows a small stream. On reaching meadowland in the valley bottom, turn left through the settlement of Champex d'en Haut.

▢ Walk past a series of barns, chalets and farmhouses, following the stream as far as Champex d'en Bas.

▢ Cross the riverside meadows, taking care not to flatten unmown grass, and reach the valley road.

▢ Turn right along this almost traffic-free road and follow it all the way back Champex.

THE ENGADINE

Maps

Landeskarte der Schweiz (1:50,000 series) Sheet 5013 — Oberengadin — Engadin' Ota

How to get there:

Road:

1   South by the European motorway system to Basel, then south-east to Zürich and Chur. South over the Julier Pass to St Moritz.
2   Via the Black Forest to Lake Constance (Bodensee). South along the Rhine valley to Chur and the Julier Pass.

Rail:

Main line Trans-European Service to Zürich and Chur, then branch line via Bever.

Air:

International airport at Zürich. Connections by rail or the local air strip at Samedan in the Engadine valley.

The Area

The famous and sophisticated who need to be seen enjoying their leisure have made St Moritz and nearby Pontresina their winter sports playground. Luxury hotels dot the sunny slopes of the valley sides, and are mostly beyond the pocket of the less favoured. St Moritz was 'discovered' by pleasure-seeking Edwardian travellers, and there is still a certain atmosphere of this bygone era about the place. Between the two world wars, skiing was very much an English affair; with only rudimentary ski tows available, the sport was a more gentle event. It was, however, the English gentlemen who created the death-defying Cresta Run, which hurtles its way down from St Moritz to finish conveniently close to Celerina's

St Moritz with Piz Julier and Piz Albana in the background

railway station. St Moritz's casinos complete the aura of indolent wealth.

Despite the ostentation of St Moritz, the Engadine remains what it has always been, a high valley in a mountain setting. Quaint farm buildings line the fertile valley floor, and ancient churches watch over the passing of time. Steep glaciers flow down into accessible side valleys and the quiet mountain sides are covered with a dazzling array of alpine flowers. Deer may be glimpsed hiding in dark recesses of the forests, and the lucky walker will see the famed chamois, the daredevil mountaineers of Europe's Alps. Whistles are a warning that the clown of the mountains, the marmot, is nearby.

The Swiss have only one national park and this is situated in a side valley below the Ofen Pass, where the season is fairly long; from mid-June to mid-October depending on the weather. Visitors who come by car are not popular, and the best way to approach the park is by using the postbus from the main valley and then walk. There is some accommodation, but it is advisable to book well in advance if you intend making a long stay inside the park. This is a tranquil place where nature accepts man; its birds and animals can be seen, often close at hand, and untouched alpine flowers, many of them rare, bloom in their natural setting.

Trains, and the postbuses which run throughout the Upper Engadine, make ideal transport for a walker wishing to explore the region. Using this system it is possible to find easy and safe walking in all the side valleys, several leading close to the terminal moraines of jagged glaciers. Panoramic walks, made possible by the use of cable cars to gain height, can be followed without difficulty across mountain sides, all with breathtaking views of snow-clad peaks.

Useful Information

Tourist Offices

Maloja
CH 7516
Telephone: 0824 3188

Pontresina
CH 7504
Telephone: 082 66488

St Moritz
CH 7500
Telephone: 082 33147

Samedan
CH 7503
Telephone: 082 65432

Celerina
CH 7505
Telephone: 082 33966

Zuoz
CH 7524
Telephone: 082 71510

Accommodation
Ranges from high-class hotels to well-appointed campsites.

Cable Cars and Chair Lifts
St Moritz (also cable railway)
Pontresina
Pont Muragl (cable railway)
Sils
Silvaplauna/Diavolezza/Lagalb

Accessible Glaciers
Roseg, Morterasch and the Diavolezza

Railways

Bernina and Glacier Express (The Rhaetian).

Swiss National Park

National Park House,
CH 7530 Zernez
Grisons
Tel: 082 81378

Road Passes

Julier	7,496ft (2,284m)
Maloja	5,924ft (1,805m)
Bernina	7,624ft (2,323m)
Albana	7,562ft (2,304m)
Fluela	7,821ft (2,383m)

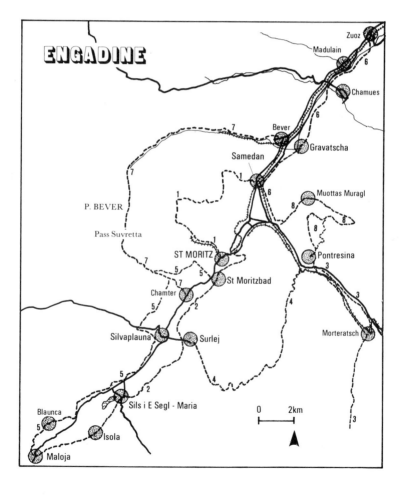

6¾ miles (10.8km), 3-4 hours. Moderate.

From a first impression gained by a quick look at the map, this might seem to be rather a hard walk for an introduction to a new area. Certainly it is over higher ground, and probably has more changes in height than most of the other introductory walks covered by this guide, but most of the initial climbing is by the Corviglia funicular which gains the initial 2,179ft (604m) needed to reach the start.

The path away from the Corviglia funicular crosses a series of high alpine pastures, northwards, beneath the enfolding arms of rocky peaks and ridges above Val Saluver. Turning eastwards, the contour — following track is a perfect viewpoint for the spectacular scenery of the Bernina and Palü ranges. This therefore is the purpose of the walk; to be able to view the whole region in one glance. Nowhere else is there such an opportunity to see the whole of the eastern Engadine in one complete view.

Turning the shoulder of Piz Padella, the path climbs to meet the track, out of Val Valletta, and this is followed to Samedan, where convenient buses and trains return to holiday bases.

The Route

□ Take the funicular railway from St Moritz to Corviglia; follow the short path towards the Piz Nair cable way.

□ Walk past the lower station of the Piz Nair cable, following a path which bears slightly right and to the north-west, away from the station.

□ Walk uphill to a footpath junction. Continue ahead by the same course, ignoring a path off to the right.

□ Climb gently around the lower slopes of Piz Nair into the rock-filled combe between Piz Nair and Piz Schlattain.

□ Fork right across a marshy area which has the Schlattain stream flowing through its middle.

□ Contour beneath Sass Corviglia and walk across high alpine pasture to a series of streams which drain the head of Val Saluver.

The combe at the head of Val Saluver offers a fine hunting ground for lovers of alpine flowers. The carline thistle and alpine anemones are fairly widespread. Marmots will be heard by their warning whistles, even if they are not seen. Silent walking might even be rewarded by glimpses of the timid chamois crossing grassy terraces between rock outcrops.

☐ Turn right at the small pool below point 2632 and continue to follow a more or less level path across the rock-strewn alpine pastures.

☐ Follow the upper edge of a rock outcrop and go under the Trais Fluors ski-tow cable.

☐ Still following a level path, cross the deep-cut ravine of Val dal Selin and continue across the hillside on the terraced path as far as point 2441.

The Engadine is spread out beneath this point. The main valley runs from right to left; opposite is Val Bernina and above it tower the Bernina, Morteratsch and Palü peaks with their surrounding glaciers.

☐ Walk on from point 2441 across the steep hillside to a footpath junction and turn left.

☐ Climb steeply uphill by a series of zigzags then by easier gradient across the lower rocky slopes of Piz Padella.

☐ Move slightly downhill, into the Valletta valley, to a footpath junction. Turn right and walk downhill as far as point 2233.

☐ Turn right, away from the main track, and walk steeply downhill in a series of zigzags into the welcome shade of the pine forest.

☐ Turn right on reaching a woodland stream and walk into Samedan by way of its upper fields.

The architecture of the old Samedan buildings is typical of the Engadine. Housing at least two families, the houses have broad roofs to withstand heavy snowfalls in winter, but perhaps the most eyecatching feature will be the heraldic designs, known as 'sgraffito', painted on the main walls of the buildings.

---

13 miles (21km), 6 hours. Easy/moderate.

Here is an ideal walk for a hot day. The shores of the treelined lakes filling the upper Engadine valley are just made for idle strolling or picnicking. Although the walk described follows the length of the valley and passes by the southern shores of each of the four lakes, or *lej* as they are known in the local Romansch language, it is not essential to complete it in one day. Conveniently-spaced access roads between lakes enable this pleasurable excursion to be spread over several days if necessary.

Strong summer sunshine warms the lake waters, and a picnic with a bathe is a pleasant combination. Whatever the plans, the walk should be one of pure enjoyment.

The route, which begins in the fashionable resort of St Moritz, follows the lake shores on a series of well-made paths. Villages, with their cafés and gasthofs along the way, mean that it will be possible to break for refreshments at convenient intervals throughout the length of the walk. The route follows the lakes all the way to the village of Maloja at the head of the valley. Check the times of local buses along the valley before setting out.

The Route

□ Cross the road behind the station complex in St Moritz and turn right down to the shore of Lej da San Murezzan (San Murezzan is Romansch for St Moritz).

□ Follow the lake side path to its forested southern shore. Continue as far as St Moritz Bad. Walk along the main road through the town.

□ Follow the road past the sports complex and along the riverside to a point about 30yd (27m) beyond a road junction, a little way beyond the Signal cable lift.

□ Turn left, slightly away from the river, to cross a series of fields. Move to the right, back towards the river bank and around the foot of a small wooded hill.

□ Follow the river, upstream, along the pine-shaded bank.

□ Cross an area of open fields to reach the Silvaplauna to Surlej road.

□ Turn left at the road, following it as far as a little bridge at right angles away from the road, over a side stream. Follow a farm lane from this bridge and across meadowland.

□ Enter along stretch of woodland and follow the southern shore of Lej da Silvaplauna all the way to Sils i E Segl - Maria. (Refreshments).

The river, which is the source of the famous Austrian Inn, can be crossed at either end of Lake Silvaplauna, which shortens the walk. Buses run along the Engadine valley back to St Moritz.

□ Follow the sharply-angled street and turn left at the eastern end of the village. A lane runs beneath a steep wooded slope; follow it until it meets a path along Lej da Segl.

□ Following the track across an alluvial fan, make for the hamlet of Isola.

The broad fan-shaped field, swampy at one end from the delta of the stream, is formed by the debris washed down Val Fedoz. The debris originated in rocks ground off the high crags of the Piz Fora ridges.

□ Follow the track, away from Isola, back towards the lakeshore, at first across rocky ground and then through a scattered belt of pine forest as far as Maloja.

□ Return to St Moritz by postbus.

The pass above Maloja has for centuries been an important communicating link between the valleys of the Inn, which flows through Switzerland and Austria into the Danube. The other river is the Maira, a swift flowing tributary of the Italian River Po. The Maloja Pass is, therefore, a link between Central Europe and Italy.

The lake at St Moritz

---

12 miles (19.3km), 6 hours. Moderate — 1,982ft (600m) ascent.

By following the well-made footpath beneath the west wall of the Morteratsch valley, and along the lateral moraine dumped by the shrinking glacier, it is possible to reach a high vantage point beneath the towering giants of the Bernina group. The complex system of glaciers flows as a frozen waterfall, and the crevassed ice-fall of the lower Morteratsch may be examined from the safety of the path. Towering over this bewildering array of snow and ice is Piz Palü — 12,816ft (3,905m); known also as the Glass Mountain, its graceful spire has been the subject of novels and romantic films. The Swiss-Italian border follows the mountain, which is a natural barrier, impenetrable to all except the most highly skilled mountaineers.

To reach the start of this walk, take the Rhaetian cog railway via Pontresina to the Morteratsch station and simply walk up the valley as far as the footpath or energy will allow. Return the same way to Morteratsch, and either catch the train back or, as suggested below, cross the Bernina valley to follow a woodland path all the way back to Pontresina.

Warning: When examining glaciers, especially near their terminal ice fall, do not wander from the marked path. Glaciers are dangerous places: they have hidden crevasses, and loose rocks drop from the ice-falls without warning!

The Route

□ Take the train to Morteratsch and turn right outside the station.

□ Climb steeply on a rocky track, through pine forest into the Morteratsch valley.

□ Beyond the upper limits of the small forest, the angle of the hillside track eases and the path follows a steadily climbing route along the west side of the valley.

Rocks and other debris have been dumped by the retreating glacier, and also by spring floodwaters from rapidly melting snow.

□ Continue along the valley as far as the Boval mountain hut — 8,189ft (2,495m). Refreshments are available.

Opposite the hut and across the glacier, a steep north-sloping ridge cleaves between the Morteratsch and the Pers Glaciers. To its left, as you face the ridge, rises Piz Palü with the Bellavista ridge connecting it to Piz Argient. Moving west, but mostly screened by its outliers, is Piz Bernina – 13,288ft (4,049m): the highest peak in the region.

North of the Pers glacier, in the north-facing combe below Munt Pers, is Diavolezza, a famous skiing area.

☐ Walk up the valley beyond the hut as far as safety and ability allows.

View the upper glacier, especially the wildly-crevassed and aptly named Labyrinth Ice Falls below Sass dal Pos.

☐ Return by the same path as far as the station.

☐ Unless returning by train, follow the path away from the station and parallel to the railway line, towards the opposite side of the Bernina valley.

☐ Join the valley road at the lower of two sharp bends. Turn right uphill on the first, and then left, away from the road, at the second.

☐ Follow a gently inclining path into mature pine forest.

☐ Cross a sparsely-wooded avalanche zone.

The open space is a good viewpoint for the Bernina peaks and their glaciers.

☐ Re-enter the forest to climb a little further before descending gradually, parallel to the road, all the way into the outskirts of Pontresina.

☐ Catch either the bus or train from the station which is across the valley, opposite the town.

Pontresina vies with neighbouring St Moritz for the standards of its high-class hotels, catering for the glittering upper echelons of society. The Romanesque church with its painted murals is worth visiting, as is the twelfth-century Spaniola tower which defended the lower valley in olden times.

VAL ROSEG FROM THE CORVATSCH CABLE WAY **4**

8 miles (12.8km), 4-5 hours. Moderate — 3,220ft (981m) descent.

The Silvaplauna-Surlej cable way takes all the effort out of any climbing involved in this walk. Using the cableway for the initial lift means that the walk can start 2,921ft (890m) above the Engadine valley, leaving a climb on foot of 184ft (56m) along an easy path to the Fuorcla Surlej Pass — 9,042ft (2,755m). A well-designed path follows the safest route down the eastern slopes of Munt Arlas — 10,263ft (3,127m), into Val Roseg where an easy track follows the river down to Pontresina station.

The actual walking starts away from the middle station of the cable way, at Murtel, but most walkers will want to go to the top of the final stage before starting the walk. This is Corvatsch, and at 10,814ft (3,295m), it is a superb vantage point from which to view all the Bernina peaks, which spread out almost a stone's throw across the intervening ridges.

Val Roseg, with its quiet forested glades, is in marked contrast to the high altitude scenery and it makes a pleasant end to this high-level excursion.

If travelling by postbus to Silvaplauna-Surlej, try to book an inclusive bus and cable car ticket as it usually saves money.

The Route

□ Take the Covatschbahn cable car from Silvaplauna-Surlej to the middle station (Murtel).

If taking the second and upper stage to Corvatsch return to Murtel to start the walk.

The top station is set on a narrow ridge between two steep glaciers on the north face of Piz Murtel – 11,267ft (3,433m).

□ From Murtel station, follow a level path eastwards across a broad scree-filled combe towards the series of crags on its far side.

□ Climb by easy zigzags over rocks to the Fuorcla Surlej pass at 9,042ft (2,755m), the highest point on the footpath.

The view across the upper Roseg valley is of the shapely ice peak of Piz Bernina – 13,289ft (4,040m) – and the steep, deeply-crevassed glaciers which flow from its north wall. Nearby satellites and their connecting ridges support Piz Bernina on all sides. To your right in the valley bottom is a glacier lake at the foot of the Roseg glacier.

□ Following a signposted route and waymarks, start to walk into Val Roseg.

The path zigzags downhill, at first over rocky ground, but later grass makes its appearance and alpine flowers are in abundance.

□ Pass the remote farm of Alp Surovel at point 2255.

□ Meet the treeline and walk down through an area of sparse pine forest to the Val Roseg Hotel (refreshments).

□ Turn left away from the hotel along its access track. Follow it along the river bank to point 1943.

□ Leave the road and turn right on a forest path paralleling both road and river.

□ Continue through mature pine forest as far as the railway line.

□ Cross the track and walk on until you reach the station road and turn left to reach Pontresina station.

□ Frequent trains return to the Engadine holiday resorts.

Walking in the Lower Engadine

---

12 miles (19km), 6-7 hours. Moderate.

By using a series of linking footpaths from the top of the Signal cableway, this delightful ramble, known as the Via Engiadina, has been created. The path begins at a high level and follows an easy contour-hugging route across Val Suvretta, keeping its height more or less all the way to Val Guglia (Julier). Skirting the lower crags of the Piz Lagret, a mountain range which makes the steep north-western wall of the upper Engadine, the path follows an easy route down through ancient pine forest, skirting the road and lakes all the way to Maloja at the head of the Engadine valley.

Hard walkers may consider an optional extension to the route which is to follow the path uphill from Samedan (the reverse of the first walk in this section), and continue beyond Corviglia to Signal. Conversely, more leisurely walkers might prefer to split the Via Engiadina, as described below, into several days of easier walking. Side paths, which can either be used to shorten the walk or for refreshment stops, connect with the valley road and its convenient bus service.

The path is waymarked throughout by a distinctive blue and yellow block symbol.

As a moneysaver, book a through ticket for both the bus and cable car, which of course can include the return journey from Maloja.

The Route

□ Use the Signal cable car to reach its upper station from St Moritz Bad, or walk up to this point from Samedan.

□ Follow the track signposted to the left (south-west) away from the upper station and across the hillside. Follow the blue and yellow waymarks.

□ Fork right at the track junction and walk round the brow of the hill into Val Suvretta.

□ Turn left at Alp Suvretta and walk downstream along the stream's left bank.

□ Turn right at a clump of trees, follow the signposted and waymarked path across the stream and uphill beneath a steep rocky outcrop.

Climb the rough hillside below tiers of crags to point 2209.

□ The path follows a level course at the foot of a steep crag. Turn left at a fork and walk down, by a zigzag path, into forest and join the Julier Pass road in Val Guglia.

The Julier Pass, which is high up on the right, connects the Engadine with the Grisons. The local Romansch spelling of the name is Gulia.

□ Turn left along the road into Samedan.

□ Walk through the village. (Refreshments).

□ Cross the river and immediately turn right. Follow the path back uphill and into the forest.

□ Turn left at a path junction above a small crag.

□ Walk slightly uphill along the forest path and keep left at the next junction.

□ Downhill through a clearing, almost as far as the road.

□ Turn right uphill and climb above a rocky outcrop.

Opposite is the village of Sils. (Refreshments).

□ Walk down to the road again, following it for about 22yd (20m) and turn right, away from the road, uphill across a steep field and into the forest.

□ Following the blue and yellow waymarks, cross the wooded rocky hillside. Fork right at the next footpath junction.

□ Over scree and turf to the alpine meadows of the Grevasalvas farmsteads.

This farm settlement is of typical Engadine timber farm houses.

□ Walk through the settlement and out along its access track, passing the farmsteads of Blaunca on the way.

□ Downhill as far as the River En. Cross the little bridge and re-enter the pine forest.

□ Follow the woodland track down to Maloja. (Refreshments and buses).

8½ miles (14km), 4-5 hours. Easy.

The Upper and Lower sections of the Engadine valley are sharply divided by the steep, forested hillside which rises dramatically between Celerina and St Moritz. Made from harder rock than the lower valley, this larch-clad eminence is used for the course of the world-famous Cresta Run. Sledges of all sizes from single to streamlined, multimanned giants, hurtle down the terrifyingly steep icy track between St Moritz and the level fields above Celerina. The hazardous sport started in the pre-war era, and the skills involved have increased to almost impossible limits.

Broad fields fill the sunny lower valley between Samedan and Zuoz, where the walk begins. The route follows easy farm lanes, with conveniently-situated villages to offer tempting refreshment stops. The finish can either be at Samedan or at Punt Muragl at the mouth of the Val Bernina.

With the railway and road always close at hand across the valley, the length of the walk should be varied at will, and can therefore be saved for either a rest or a rainy day.

The Route

□ The walk begins from Zuoz railway station. Walk down the road and over the river.

Zuoz, an unspoilt village away from the busier tourist centres, is a delightful grouping of the typical Engadine style of houses. In the main square, a fountain is surmounted by the heraldic bear of the local Planta family. Their arms include a severed bear's paw with sole or planta upwards.

The Crusch-Alva Inn, dating from 1570, is on the main street. The parish church of St Luzius, dominated by its slender spire, has a particularly interesting nave roof. The Planta family's bear paw theme keeps recurring in the interior decoration.

□ Turn right at the riverside farm of Resgia and walk along a farm track through lush meadowland and other farm fields close by the River Inn.

The wide Inn valley has to be protected from flooding. The path follows the top of the raised bank.

The village square at Zuoz

☐ Follow the river below Madulain village (refreshments), as far as the La Punt to Chamues-ch road.

☐ Cross the road, walk between a row of houses and over a canalised side-stream then out onto the main river's bank. Follow it upstream until the path moves away to the left to circumvent a boggy area near Gravatscha.

☐ Walk along the lower boundary of the forested hillside, following it back towards the river.

☐ Join a track along the western edge of the Engadine airport. Turn right at the airport buildings if intending to go to Samedan, either to finish the walk or for refreshments: **otherwise:**

☐ Go straight on beyond the airport along a narrow lane towards the railway.

☐ Turn left, away from the railway and walk towards the forest edge by the Acla-Bardun farm.

☐ Walk, by easy gradients, uphill through pine forest, swinging right towards a multi-path junction.

☐ Bear right on a minor track, downhill towards the Muottas Muragl funicular.

☐ Go over the funicular track by a bridge and almost immediately cross a small stream.

☐ Turn right and then left paralleling the stream to follow a path between a group of chalets.

☐ Join the valley road at Punt Muragl. The railway station is on the right.

16 miles (25.7km), 8 hours. Strenuous — 2,977ft (907m) ascent.

This is a long hard walk, but one which should be within the capabilities of anyone who has followed most of the other walks in this area. The climbing is gradual, and the sense of achievement on reaching the top of the climb to Pass Suvretta will be compensation for all the effort involved in walking up the Bever valley.

The walk starts at Bever and follows the gradual incline of the valley all the way to Zembers da Suvretta on Alp Suvretta. The way forks at this point and is the only section with any steep climbing; fortunately not long. Val Suvretta da Samedan is followed to its head and once over the pass the flooded hollow of Lej Suvretta soon comes into view.

Beyond the lake the walking is all downhill, following the Murezzan version of the Suvretta valley. It is a little confusing to find similarly named valleys on either side of a pass, but the answer lies in the word Suvretta, which is obviously some ancient Romansch word to describe the shape of the valley.

The Route

□ The walk starts at Bever. Follow the side road out of the village, westwards into Val Bever.

□ At the point where the road crosses the river opposite the railway, turn right, away from the river (ie do not cross the river), and walk along a cart track, over a field and towards a clump of pines.

□ Walk through the small area of woodland, then out through a series of meadows below the main forest's edge.

□ Pass a number of small farms, gradually climbing towards the Spinas railway station at the southern end of the tunnel complex on the Rhaetian line from Chur.

□ Turn right above and away from the station and follow the footpath across the tunnel portal, then down to and over a small stream.

□ Turn right at the forest edge, walk across a small alpine meadow to the farmstead of Prasüratsch.

□ Continue up the valley by following a jeep track in and out of sparse pine woodland, at the side of an increasingly rocky hillside.

□ The jeep track ends at the Palud Marscha farm.

□ Follow a footpath beyond the farm buildings across level alpine pastures.

□ Cross the river at point 2104 and follow the right bank (the river should be on your right if you are walking upstream).

□ Reach Alp Suvretta, which is an excellent area for alpine flowers.

□ Turn left just before the group of barns and old buildings which make up Zembers da Suvretta.

□ Walk steeply uphill towards, then alongside, the stream in the valley of Suvretta da Samedan.

□ Above point 2379 the angle of ascent eases a little, but the ground is stonier although still firm underfoot.

□ Climb to Pass Suvretta — 8,582ft (2,615m).
The view across upper Engadine is of the Bernina group.

□ Walk down to Lej Suvretta.
The lake makes an ideal picnic spot, and although icy-cold it is suitable for swimming.

□ Follow the out-flowing stream on a path which wanders between rocky outcrops and over springy turf, gradually downhill through Suvretta de San Murezzan.

□ Fork right at Alp Suvretta, still following the stream downhill.

□ Enter a narrow wooded ravine. Fork right near point 1993 to follow a streamside path, all the way to the valley road at Champfer. There is a frequent bus service to St Moritz and beyond.

View from Muottas Muragl ▷

LAKE MURAGL

---

7 miles (11km), 3-4 hours. Moderate.

This is a short day's walk, included as a possibility for the last day of a holiday in Engadine; it is ideally suited for a final visit to the high mountains. A simple walk, easy to follow with very little uphill climbing, the climax is a pretty lake set at the foot of the tiered crags of Piz Vadret — 10,499ft (3,199m), which could be scaled by a suitably competent party, by way of the Fuorcla Muragl col, an easy climb above the lake.

By using the Muottas Muragl funicular from Punt Muragl, one can avoid climbing something like 2,347ft (715m). Beyond the upper station, an easy path slants upward beneath the Tschimas ridge, an outlier of Piz Vadret, to reach Lake Muragl. Following its outflowing stream, the path leaves the upper valley, then for this walk swings left around the broad western shoulder of Las Sours, before zigzagging through the forest down to Pontresina.

If travelling by bus or train from another point in the Engadine valley to Punt Muragl, try to book a through, or 'Hiker's' ticket, to the top of the Muottas Muragl funicular.

The Route

☐ Take the funicular from Punt Muragl to the top of the Muottas Muragl.

☐ Turn right, away from the upper station and follow an easy path to the Muottas alpine farm.

Muottas Muragl is a good viewpoint for the upper Engadine and the peaks surrounding the Julier Pass. Beneath and to the right, the River Inn flows north-eastwards towards the Austrian border.

☐ Fork left at the farmstead, uphill, past a wooden barn. Gradually contour to the right beneath the outcropping rocks of the Tschimas ridge.

☐ The angle of ascent eases the closer one gets to the upper valley.

☐ Descend slightly to the small lake of Lej Muragl.

Lej Muragl makes an ideal picnic spot. Above it the rocky screes are often crossed by chamois, and around the lake, especially in sheltered corners, a fine selection of alpine flowers bloom in summer.

☐ Follow the shoreline round as far as the outflow. Walk downstream on the right bank leaving the rocky higher valley for more stable vegetation in the lower hollow.

☐ At a footpath junction, turn left across the stream, then immediately right at a fork.

There is an optional diversion from this point which would make a longer and higher level walk by way of the Segantini hut. (Refreshments). Rejoining the rest of the walk at the path junction near point 2231, as described below.

☐ Contour left around the hillside beneath a prominent crag and walk to the mountain farm of Munt da la Bês-cha. (Refreshments).

☐ Ignore the path downhill to the right at point 2335.

☐ Begin to descend, working across the steep hillside on a well-maintained path.

☐ Immediately above the treeline at point 2231, turn right at a path junction and then left over rocky ground.

Good views of the Bernina group and their glaciers from point 2231.

☐ Enter the forest and walk down the steep hillside by a narrow zigzag path.

☐ Follow this forest path all the way into Pontresina. There is a regular bus service down the valley from here; the railway station is on the opposite side of the valley away from the town.

Zermatt

Maps

Landeskarte der Schweiz (1:50,000 series) Sheet 5006 — Zermatt und Umgebung.

How to get there:

Road:

1   South to Lausanne by way of Basel and Bern. Follow the Rhône valley road to Visp. Zermatt is to the south along the Mattertal Valley.

2   As above as far as Bern then south to Kandersteg and take the car-ferry train to Brig. Zermatt is to the south-west via Visp.

Rail:

Main line on the trans-European system to Brig, then narrow gauge on the Brig-Visp-Zermatt railway.

Air:

International airports at Bern and Geneva. Rail connections via Brig.

The Area

The mention of the name Zermatt will probably conjure up a mental picture of timber farmhouses dominated by the soaring finger of the Matterhorn. As true as this scene may be, it is only one of the pictures offered by a magnificent range of mountains and glaciers which surround this resort.

Set at an altitude of 5,300ft (1,615m), Zermatt was only 'discovered' a little over 130 years ago by early alpinists. As the sport grew, this sleepy Valaisian village of wooden houses on their mushroom-like straddlestones sprang to fame following the disastrous first ascent of the Matterhorn by an ill-fated party led by Edward Whymper.

Schwarzsee chapel at the foot of the Matterhorn

In an area of superb scenery, it is difficult to single out any individual viewpoint as being the 'best'. Certainly those views dominated by the Matterhorn will be considered by many to be supreme, but it will be a critical viewer indeed who is not moved by the panorama of mountains viewed from the top of the Gornergrat. Peak upon peak range from the north, starting with the Bernese alps; Monte Rosa is to the east, next come the twins of Castor and Pollux; Breithorn and its near neighbour the Matterhorn crowd each other, with the Weisshorn's needle summit completing the western sweep. The foreground is far from neglected, for here the Gorner glacier and it tributaries blend into one vast, relentlessly flowing river of ice thousands of years old. To enjoy this marvellous panorama, take the electric train from Zermatt to the Gornergrat station, where a short walk leads to a viewing platform at 10,270ft

(3,130m). A fifteen-minute cable car ride from here climbs to the summit of the Stockhorn (11,175ft, 3,406m), where there is, if anything, a more impressive view.

There is a steep downhill mountain track from the Gornergrat, but this should only be attempted by more experienced walkers. The path from the Rotenboden station below Gornergrat, is perhaps more suitable for the average walker. This path also skirts the lateral moraine of the Gorner glacier near its final ice-fall. A side track leads to the Riffelberg Hotel where there will be refreshment and also the chance to use the train for the rest of the downhill journey, should the inclination arise.

One of the many attractions of Zermatt is the simple fact that it is closed to all except essential local traffic. Motorists must leave their cars at Täsch — 3 miles (5km) down the valley — and travel into Zermatt by a shuttle service. This traffic-free atmosphere makes the little town a walkers' paradise.

The possibilities for walking are only limited by the abilities of the walker. Mile after mile of well-maintained and waymarked paths lead away from Zermatt, and non-walking activities are also all that one would expect from an alpine resort; from the energetic disco to a cosy evening's entertainment in one of the local bars. It is even possible to ski throughout the summer on snow below the Klein (little) Matterhorn.

Useful Information

Tourist Office
Zermatt Tourist Office,
CH 3920 Zermatt
Telephone: 028 671031

Accommodation
All grades from single to five star rated hotels; apartments and campsites.

Cable Cars and Mountain Railways
Zermatt — Gornergrat (train)
Gornergrat — Stockhorn (cable car)
Sunnegga — Rothorn (funicular and cable car)
Zermatt — Schwarzsee (cable car)
Furgg — Trockener Steg — Klein Matterhorn (cable car)

Glacier Viewing

Gorner — from the Gornergrat Panorama platform.
Klein Matterhorn — from the Klein Matterhorn cable way.

Swimming

Most of the mountain lakes are suitable for swimming. Grünsee and Leisee are especially recommended. Indoor pools at various hotels in and around Zermatt.

Other Sports

Tennis, mini-golf, keepfit course (vita-parcours).

Sights

Alpine Museum, Cemetery, Gorner Ravine, Glacier Garden.

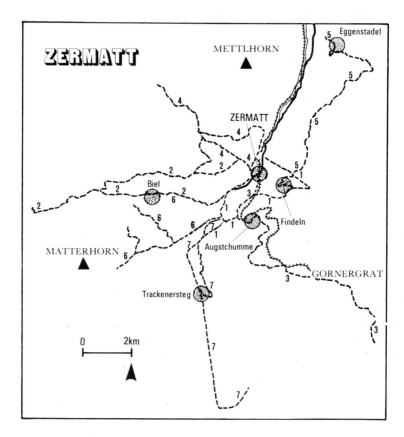

---

7 miles (11.3km), 3-4 hours. Moderate.

The focal point for everyone who visits Zermatt is going to be the stately Matterhorn — 14,690ft (4,476m); its rocky pyramid dominates the upper Mattertal valley.

There are many famous vantage points, well-recorded by photographers, but perhaps the best view of all is from Findeln. This tiny settlement of warm-hued wooden *mazots* or barns, timber farmhouses and its homely stone chapel, makes an excellent foreground to the Matterhorn.

Findeln is reached by way of an underground funicular railway from Zermatt, the Alpen-Metro Sunnegga, from which an easy downhill walk leads to the bottom of the Gornergrat glacier and its famous glacier garden.

Woodland tracks, which lead back to Zermatt, give the opportunity to explore the village and valley, so full of alpine history. The walk is designed to reach one of the best viewpoints in the alps, with the minimum effort, and also to tune up muscles jaded either from inactivity or perhaps the long journey to Switzerland.

The Route

□ Take the Alpen-Metro Sunnegga underground railway from the lower station — 5,317ft (1,620m), across the river east of the town centre, to reach Sunnegga — 7,509ft (2,288m).

Sunnegga is the middle station of a complex of funicular, gondola and cabin lifts which eventually reaches the summit of the Unterrothorn – 10, 184ft (3,103m); a peak with unimpeded views of the surrounding mountains and glaciers.

□ Turn left away from Sunnegga, ignoring the main path signposted to Findeln. Follow a minor path through the line of crags to the south and beneath Sunnegga.

□ Walk beneath a supply cable and downhill, to the narrow Lake Leisee.

The sun-warmed waters of the Leisee are suitable for swimming.

□ Walk across alpine pasture to a path junction, and turn right towards the group of wooden buildings at Eggen.

☐ Keep left, beyond the settlement, downhill past a series of timber barns to reach Findeln. (Refreshments).

This is a good place to stop and appreciate the magnificent view of the Matterhorn, and perhaps photograph it with the foreground of interesting Findeln farmhouses. It is possible to buy light meals and refreshments from Findeln.

☐ From the middle of Findeln turn left, downhill, towards and then over the stream in the valley below. Cross the bridge and turn right to follow a narrow path slanting uphill through pine forest.

☐ Cross a woodland stream and begin to descend fairly steeply as far as the Gornergrat's Findelnbach station.

☐ Follow the gravel-surfaced road to the left, away from the station, and then turn left again at its junction with a forest road. Follow this as far as a group of buildings on the east bank of the Gornera river.

☐ Turn left along the river bank, upstream, away from the pine woods on a signposted path towards the Gletschergarten (glacier garden).

The glacier garden has been made from the curious litter of boulders and smooth slabs left by the retreating Gorner glacier. Alpine plants and shrubs, unique to the area, grow in shallow but well-drained soil, sheltered in pockets between the rocks.

☐ Walk back downhill from the garden through ancient moraines as far as the treeline and the road. Turn left at the roadway.

☐ Walk past the Furi cable station across an open grassy hillside.

☐ Turn right opposite Furi church, then go downhill by footpath to the hamlet of Zum See.

☐ Follow a well-made path to the left, down a small wooded slope to the Zmuttbach river.

☐ Cross the river, climb a little way up the opposite slope, then turn right and start to walk downhill. The path follows the river all the way into the outskirts of Zermatt.

There is a good view of Zermatt from the path below Zum See.

---

16 miles (25.7km), 6 hours. Moderate/strenuous — 3,525ft (1,074m) ascent.

This walk follows the retreating Zmutt glacier all the way from its ancient junction with the Gorner glacier. The path moves through moraine deposits at the side of the valley, until on reaching the Schönbiel hut, the awesome crevasses of a still-active ice-fall can be seen at close range. All that is now left of the Zmutt (since, like most alpine glaciers, it is very much in retreat) fills the upper valley, west of Zermatt. Three major subsidiary glaciers, the Schönbiel, Stockjigle and the Tiefmatten, flow with their slow but relentless pace, beneath a cirque of peaks, beginning with the Matterhorn and ending at the Dent Blanche. All three glaciers join opposite the Schönbiel hut, which sits on a rocky eminence at the foot of a long south-facing ridge from Dent Blanche.

The walk follows the north bank of the Zmutt river all the way from Zermatt to the Schönbiel hut. On the return journey there is an optional diversion across a high alp at Hohbalmen, above a line of crags guarding the end of the valley.

The Route

□ Walk out of Zermatt towards Winkelmatten towards the Klein Matterhorn cable car lower terminus. Do not cross the river, but continue upstream along the north bank. The path is well defined.

□ Go through an area of sparse woodland and climb around the shoulder of the lower rocks on the craggy hillside.

□ Walk through the scattered summer farming alp of Zmutt, above its water-scoured ravine. (Refreshments available in Zmutt.)

Spend a little time looking at the interesting timber farmhouses and barns (mazots) in Zmutt. Cattle and goats, grazing on the surrounding pasture, spend their winters in the lower valley.

□ Climbing gradually, leave the flower speckled pasture for the start of the ancient moraines.

□ Keep right at a footpath junction to the east of a small reservoir.

□ Climb, steeply, through a break in the crag wall ahead.

□ Ignore a path to the right (this is the start of a diversion on the return section of the walk). Cross the broad, rocky mouth of a side valley, the Arben-Gandegge.

▢ On a level path, pass a small lake and continue up the valley.

▢ The path climbs at an increasingly steep angle, zigzagging for the last few hundred feet to the Schönbiel hut.

The Schönbiel is run by the Swiss Alpine Club.

Observe the views of glaciers and peaks. To the south, the Matterhorn and the Dent d'Hérens rise. Behind at the head of the Schönbiel glacier is the Dent Blanche – 14,296ft (4,356m).

It is possible to follow the path beyond the hut, even higher, and to the side of the fearsome ice-fall, but this will take at least 1½ hours and therefore both the time and your condition should be considered before going any further.

▢ To return, reverse the route unless taking the option to cross Höhbalmen.

Höhbalmen option:

▢ Turn left beyond the mouth of the side valley at Arben-Gandegge, in the above instructions and climb steeply by the broad zigzags of a narrow path.

▢ Follow this path across the wide ledge of Höhbalmen.

▢ Fork right and follow a stream steeply downhill from point 2665.

▢ Swing left across the steep hillside as far as the small pine forest above Alterhaupt. (Refreshments at the Edelweiss Gasthof).

▢ Follow a steep zigzag path down to Zermatt.

A typical Alpine restaurant near Zermatt

12½ miles (20km), 6 hours. Moderate.

Although this walk officially starts at the Rotenboden station on the Gornergrat railway, most visitors, especially those on their first visit to Zermatt, will want to take the train up to its terminus on the Gornergrat. They may even wish to continue from there, via the dual cable, to the top of the Stockhorn. Both points, the Gornergrat and Stockhorn, offer impressive views over a panorama of glacier and peaks, but the Stockhorn, being higher at 11,592ft (3,532m), has the better views. If the decision is made to visit both of these places, then time should be allowed to complete this exciting walk.

Glaciers can be dangerous places for the unwary; crevasses may lie for years beneath a route crossed by hundreds of climbers, and then one day the snow covering collapses, pitching the unlucky mountaineer into the depths. Fortunately, the route taken by this walk, across a neck of the Gornergrat glacier, has been well-probed and the marked path is over solid ice with a firm covering of hard packed snow. The walk, after leaving Rotenboden, descends a lateral moraine to reach the glacier. The return is made from the Swiss Alpine Club's Monte Rosa hut, following the same route back to Rotenboden and then descending slopes covered with alpenrose to Zermatt.

The Route

□ Take the Gornergrat funicular railway from the centre of Zermatt to the Rotenboden halt (**NB:** if continuing to the Gornergrat terminus or beyond, it is possible to walk back by footpath to Rotenboden.)

□ Follow the footpath signposted 'Gornergletscher and Monte Rosahütte', to the right and away from the station.

□ Cross a rocky hollow above three small lakes as far as point 2775.

□ Turn left and follow the well-defined path downhill, angling across the rock and scree-covered south face of the Gornergrat.

□ Walk through an area of moraine heaps, following white-red-white block waymark symbols out on to the glacier.

It may be difficult to realise that the glacier has been reached. Far from being the pure white objects they appear from a distance, they are, especially along the edges, dirty, rock-strewn places. Glare from reflected sunlight and surface water from the melting snow are likely to be the worst problems encountered, but do not stray from the marked path across the glacier.

☐ Follow the track towards a protuding mass of rocks in the middle of the glacier continue to follow the marked path.

☐ Walk round the foot of a rocky outcrop and then steeply uphill over a scree slope to the Monte Rosa hut, where refreshments are available.

This alpine setting offers views of the Matterhorn from a new angle. The peaks along the west wall of the Mattertal valley are also revealed, and range from the Dent Blanche on the left to the Zinalrothorn and the Weisshorn further right.

☐ Return by the same route across the glacier and then climb steeply uphill to point 2775 below the Rotenboden halt.

☐ Turn left and walk around three lakes, the central of which is the Riffelsee. Keep left at a path junction by this lake.

☐ Walk downhill through clumps of alpenrose beneath the Riffelhorn.

☐ Bear right beyond the top of a ski lift. Pass a small chapel to reach the hotel Riffelberg. (Refreshments).

☐ Walk downhill away from the hotel on a clearly defined path, through a craggy area, then across a deep-cut side valley; reach the scattered farm settlement of Riffelalp.

☐ Keep left away from the railway. Zigzag steeply downhill into pine forest and swing left across the mountainside to the farms at Augstschumme.

☐ Continue downhill on a zigzag path; re-enter the forest and walk towards the valley road.

☐ Turn right on the gravel-surfaced road and follow it back to Zermatt.

(10,496ft, 3,198m)

---

8 miles (12.8km), 8-9 hours. Strenuous — 5,179ft (1,578m) ascent.

This is not a walk for the faint-hearted. It is a tough climb; the angle hardly ever relents all the way from Zermatt to the hut; but for those who can complete the walk, it will give them an immense sense of achievement. From its eyrie on a ledge at the foot of the Zinalrothorn's south ridge, the Rothornhütte looks directly across the upper Mattertal valley to that huge expanse of glaciers, bounded by summits which make the border between Italy and Switzerland: a border which is impregnable to all except skilled mountaineers.

As the Rothornhütte faces east it is an ideal place to experience the beauty of an alpine dawn. An overnight stay at the hut, and a very early start the next day, is therefore suggested. Accommodation is simple, but the food is good and above all the atmosphere, as in all alpine huts, is one of friendly camaraderie.

The path to the Rothornhütte leaves Zermatt and climbs by way of Balmen above Zermatt's campsite. The path then starts the steep climb across the rocky lower slopes of the Weisshorn, to join the Trift valley above an alp of the same name. Relentlessly hard climbing, more or less all the way, is then necessary to reach the hut.

The Route

□ Follow the path behind the main railway station uphill, beyond the campsite and heliport, to the farmsteads at Balmen.

□ Climb round the bottom of a wall of crags as far as a footpath junction above the swift-flowing Luegel stream.

□ Turn left, away from the stream, and follow a marked path through a series of tiered crags to point 2503.

□ Ignore a path on the right signposted to the Mettelhorn, follow another path, now at an easier angle, across the grassy hillside.

□ Walk down into the hollow of Trift alp.

Refreshments are available at Trift, on the left, a little way below the path.

□ Turn right at a junction with the valley path. Zigzag uphill again through a line of outcropping rocks.

☐ Walk across scree-covered Vieliboden. Aim towards the steep rocky wall ahead.

☐ Turn left, across a small stream, and climb around the side of a rock wall on a waymarked path.

☐ Follow the white-red-white marks on a path which leads steeply up the scree slope to the promontory above. The Swiss flag marks the positon of the hut, and acts as a guide for the final stage of the climb.

To the left of the Rothornhütte are the smooth lower slopes of the Triftglacier, but above it towards the south wall of the Zinalrothorn – 13,853ft (4,221m) – the glacier becomes a jagged mass of ice blocks as it flows over an outcropping crag.

☐ Return from the hut, downhill through Vieliboden to the footpath junction above Trift. Turn right and walk down to the farm buildings.

☐ Turn left below the hamlet to follow the well-defined path downhill alongside the stream.

Animals and people living at Trift come up this path early in the summer, from their winter quarters in the Mattertal valley.

☐ Above a line of steep rocks, the path swings to the right bank over the stream.

☐ Turn right downhill on a zigzag route across the stream.

☐ Turn left at footpath junction near Alterhaupt and continue downhill.

☐ Turn right at a junction and walk very steeply downhill following the stream into the centre of Zermatt.

A HILLSIDE AND VALLEY WALK

---

7 miles (11.3km), 3-4 hours. Easy/moderate (optional extension :
3 miles (4.8km), 1½ hours).

Unless you are content with gentle pottering on short level tracks, walking in the Zermatt area tends to be of a strenuous nature. Steep valley sides and attractive, almost inaccessible viewpoints, make their demands on enthusiastic walkers who visit this area. As all the previous walks have been demanding of both time and energy, the following walk has been included as a contrast. The walk can be used on an afternoon when other plans or activities prevent a full day's high-level walking, or perhaps to fill a more relaxing day.

Using the underground funicular railway to reach Sunnegga, an easy path is then followed, just above the treeline to Tufteren. The route proceeds along a less well used path over the north-west ridge of Sattelspitz to reach Täschalp, a remote farming area in the Mellichbach valley. Downhill walking finishes the mountain section and at Täsch the decision either to return to Zermatt by train or follow the riverside track back to the village must be made.

The Route

☐ Climb to Sunnegga by the Alpen-Metro from Zermatt.

☐ Turn left, down-valley, away from the upper station and walk through a natural gap in the lower crag.

☐ Cross a grassy slope, skirting the upper limits of the pine forest.

☐ Walk through short stretches of forest to reach Tufteren alpine settlement. (Refreshments).

☐ Fork right on leaving the hamlet and move away from the main path. Climb the hillside towards an area of rock and scree.

☐ At a fork on the far side of the scree bear left to continue along the same contour.

☐ Climb by path round the upper part of a deep rocky ravine.

☐ Follow the path beyond the ravine on a reasonably level course, towards the main ridge which will be seen about 1½ miles (2.4km) ahead.

☐ Walk across a scree slope and then climb to the right and join a path which has climbed the hillside on the left. Turn right on this new path and cross the rocky ridge.

□ Walk down the slope through bands of rock and scree into the Mellichbach valley. (Refreshments).

The hill settlements of Ottavan and Stafelti are quite untouched by tourism, and retain many unique examples of the local high-level farm architecture.

□ Follow the track north-west away from Stafelti around the wooded shoulder of the hill.

□ Ignoring minor paths, follow the main track as it swings from side to side down the valley.

□ Cross the stream, leaving the forested area to walk through the settlements of Resti and Täschberg to reach the village of Täsch in the main valley. (Refreshments).

Optional extension:

□ Cross the Mattervispa river beyond Täsch and turn left, upstream, past the campsite.

□ Follow the riverside track to a group of barns at Zermattjen. Turn right, away from the river and follow the railway line beneath the rocky crags of Ausserberg, on the lower slopes of the Mettelhorn, all the way back to Zermatt.

The cable cars to Furi and the Schwarzsee

10 miles (16km), 7-8 hours. Strenuous — 2,222ft (677m) — ascent, 5,382ft (1,640m) descent.

The story of the tragic first ascent of the Matterhorn led by the young British illustrator Edward Whymper, is well known. After eight attempts from Breuil on the Italian side (the Italians call the mountain Monte Cervino), he switched his approach to the Swiss side above Zermatt. What subsequently followed was, by today's mountaineering safety standards, sheer ineptitude. A rope of low breaking strength connected a team of inexperienced climbers, all moving unbelayed, ie not anchored to the rock face. One of them fell, dragging three others and a local guide to their deaths 4,000ft (1,200m) below. The fact that two crosses shone in the clouds (a natural phenomenon) soon afterwards, helped to romanticise the disaster and ensure that it remains a macabre piece of alpine history.

The route follows Whymper's footsteps as far as the Hörnli hut. Built long after his ascent, it is now used as the base camp for aspiring latter day mountaineers. Returning from the Hörnli, the path crosses the slopes of the Stafelalp to reach forested valleys in the Matterhorn's shadow.

Make an early start, as there is no shade on the higher sections of this walk and the sun can be strong at high altitudes.

This walk is only suitable for adequately equipped and experienced hill walkers. There is a moderate amount of scrambling involved on the exposed ridge. A good head for heights is essential.

The Route

☐ Take the cable car from Winkelmatten by way of Furi to the Schwarzsee lake.

The lake is over a slight rise to the west beyond the upper station. It fills a hollow carved by an ancient glacier, which also honed the nearby rounded slabs. On a day with no wind, the lake mirrors the nearby peaks and, with the mountain chapel of St Mary of the Snow, the scene is such that the temptation to stay and photograph it must be great. However, time is limited and the way to the Hörnli hut is long and tiring!

☐ Take the left fork above the cable way and follow the white-red-white waymarks signposted to the Hörnlihutte.

□ Walk past the Schwarzsee and climb a low crag by the waymarked path.

□ Cross the sparsely-grassed upper slopes beyond the crag and then by a short scree slope reach a second and larger crag. Climb this by the marked zigzag route.

□ Skirt the upper edge of the Furgg glacier, seen curving to the left below the Hörnli ridge, the object of the walk.

□ Ahead is a rocky wall which towers above the screes and moraines of the upper glacier. Follow the path towards it and then left as far as a natural gap in the crag.

□ Climb the crag by easy steps, to the right and then left, out on to the ridge itself.

□ The angle of the ridge now increases and the path follows a zigzag route marked with white-red-white blocks for about 1¼ miles (2km), during which it is necessary to climb some 1,280ft (390m), over increasingly rocky ground on a narrow ridge.

Take great care on this section. Do not dislodge any rocks which may fall on other climbers.

□ Reach the Hörnli hut. The final 3,988ft (1,215m) to the top of the Matterhorn towers dizzily above the hut. The ridge appears to rise vertically from this vantage point.

Do not stay overnight at the Hörnli, unless you do not mind overcrowding and being woken up early by climbers attempting the summit.

□ Return by the same route as far as the Schwarzsee. (Refreshments). **NB:** ignore a minor path to the left, below point 2960 on the Hörnli ridge.

□ Turn left away from the upper station and restaurant, walk downhill by a path across an area of rugged sparsely-grassed hillside, with a remarkable variety of alpine flowers.

□ Follow the path all the way to Stafel (signposted), a hill settlement immediately above the treeline. (Refreshments).

□ Walk downhill again from Stafel into forest and turn right along a track past the Biel farms.

□ Continue along the track into the Zmutt valley and join the reservoir access road. Turn right for about ¼ mile (400m) and then left, across the river to the group of farms and chalets at Zmutt.

□ Follow the rocky path into the main valley, through sparse woodland into meadows leading to the outskirts of Zermatt.

THE KLEIN MATTERHORN

(12,744ft, 3,883m)

4½ miles (7.2km), 3 hours. Moderate — 4,329ft (1,319m) —
descent from Trockenersteg

If the Matterhorn is well beyond the capabilities of the average hill
walker, then the Klein (or little) Matterhorn is a consolatory
expedition. There is a four-stage cable car system which finishes
directly on the summit of this mountain.

Here anyone with a love of mountains will appreciate the world
of rock and ice, which apart from the man-made intrusions
connected with the cable car and its attendant buildings, has
remained virtually unchanged since the last ice age. Most of Europe
looked like this at that time; alpine glaciers are now only a small
reminder of the massive ice sheet which once filled the valleys and
covered the lower mountains.

The walk described here is in two sections; the first is a short
excursion from the top of the Klein Matterhorn across the
Breithorn Plateau, the upper junction of a complex system of
glaciers. Returning by cable car to the Trockenersteg station, the
second and longer part of the walk makes its way in easy stages to
the Gorner ravine and then returns to Zermatt by a shady forest
track.

Sunglasses, long-sleeved shirts and barrier creams are essential
safeguards against the intense glare of sunlight reflected from the
glacier.

The Route

☐ Take the four stages of the Klein Matterhorn cable car system
from Winkelmatten to the summit. The intermediate stations are at
Furi, Furgg and Trockenersteg.

☐ Follow the marked track south, away from the rocky summit out
on to the glacier.

*It is possible to follow the glacier track to the snow-capped summit
of the Breithorn, 13,666ft (4,164m). Check at the upper station if the
track is currently open and safe.*

NB: *remember that the air at this altitude is thin and low in oxygen.
Do not rush; walk at a much slower pace than normal. Even though you
may feel fit, altitude sickness can strike without warning.*

□ Return by cable car to Trockenersteg. (Refreshments).

□ Turn right away from the station, downhill over a rough scree-covered slope and also a small stream, to join the path from the nearby Gandegg hut. (Refreshments).

□ Turn left along this well-marked path, across the broad rocky hillside and out on to steep sparsely-grassed slopes above the terminal moraines of the Gorner glacier.

The glacier stretches away to the east, to the frontier ridge. The Gornergrat with its railway is opposite, and to the right at the head of the glacier is the Monte Rosa massif – 14,946ft (4,554m), the highest peak in the area.

□ Zigzag steeply downhill to the Furgg gorge.

□ Cross the gorge and its river by a well-maintained track. Turn right and climb the rocky slope opposite.

□ Follow the descending path across scree-covered slabs and the boulderfield as far as the treeline.

□ Walk through a belt of pines and out on to meadows near the hamlet of Furi.

An optional diversion to the glacier garden can be taken by following a signposted path from Furi.

□ Turn right through its scattered farms and chalets to reach the access road.

□ Follow the access road back to Zermatt, using short-cut paths where signposted, to avoid wide sweeping bends in the road.

SHORT WALKS AROUND ZERMATT

There are a number of easy valley strolls around the village and along its main or side valleys. None of them need take more than a couple of hours to complete and they are, therefore, suitable for an off day or perhaps an after-dinner walk. The following selection are just an indication of what can be done; some of the walks can be linked into longer tours as time or inclination dictates.

From Zermatt

Winkelmatten and Zum See $3\frac{1}{2}$ miles (5.6km), $1\frac{3}{4}$ hours. A stroll through meadow and woodland along an easy gradient to a group of farms and an alpine restaurant.

Winkelmatten — Moos — Blatten 2 miles (3.2km), 1 hour. Easy woodland walking.

Gorner ravine $4\frac{1}{2}$ miles (7.2km), 2 hours. Mountain road and well-maintained path to roaring waterfalls.

Täsch $4\frac{1}{2}$ miles (7.2km), 2 hours. Easy descent, partly through woodland and over meadows. Closely follows the river for most of the way. Return by train.

Ried $2\frac{1}{2}$ miles (4km), 2 hours. An easy woodland stroll. Gasthofs in Houeten and Ried.

From the Gornergrat Railway (GGB)

Riffelalp to Grünsee 4 miles (6.4km), 2 hours. Level path through larch and pine woods to a glacial lake.

Riffelalp An ideal place for a picnic; covered with alpine flowers, especially alpenrose in June and July.

From Sunnegga

Leisee Picnicking and bathing.

Seelisee 2 miles (3.2km), 2 hours. Lakes and alpine valley scenery. Access by a moderately steep path from the Blauherd gondola lift.

Tufteren $2\frac{1}{2}$ miles (4km), $1\frac{1}{2}$ hours. Easy, contour-following path to mountain farms. Gasthof.

SAAS-FEE

Maps

Landeskarte der Schweiz (1:50,000 series). Sheet 274 – Visp, Sheet 284 – Mischabel and Saas-Fee (1: 25,000) Wanderkarte Saastal.

How to get there:

Road:

1   South through Lausanne and Sion, followed by the Rhône Valley route to Visp, then south by minor road to Saas-Fee.

2   Alternatively, south from Bern to Speiz and Kandersteg, then car transporter train to Brig and via Visp as route 1.

Rail:

1   Via Geneva and the Brig train by way of Lausanne and Martigny. Connections to Visp and the postbus to Saas-Fee.

2   Via Bern and Kandersteg to Brig. Local train or bus to Visp then postbus as above.

The Area

Tucked away in a side valley beneath towering snow-clad peaks and steep glaciers, at a first glance Saas-Fee would hardly seem to be suitable for summer walking holidays. Certainly its situation makes it an ideal ski resort, for which of course it is better known. Thanks to its very position, and with its carefully contrived tracks running for miles across the lower slopes of the 'home' mountains, there is more than enough scope for the most discerning walker.

Saas-Fee is geared to the pedestrian; cars are not allowed into the village and must park in one of the two conveniently sited car parks, neither of which are very far from the village centre, its hotels or the campsite. Without doubt it is this freedom from the domination of the motor car which helps to make the charming village of Saas-Fee an ideal spot for mountain walkers. Of course the fact that it is a suntrap, with magnificent high alpine scenery so close at hand cannot be discounted, but the freedom from motor vehicles is such a unique pleasure that it can take a few days fully to appreciate.

There are something like 174 miles (280km) of well-engineered and carefully waymarked footpaths in this area, ranging from one-hour valley walks to ambitious full-day high-level tours. Tracks across the forested slopes offer hours of cool walking with unexpected views, either of the valley or of distant peaks glimpsed through gaps between the trees.

Cableways and even an underground railway take most of the effort out of high-level climbing. All lead to outstandingly beautiful panoramic views of mountains and glaciers. From the Hannig cableway it is possible to see occasional groups of chamois and that

Saas-Fee

151

monarch of the alps, the ibex, a spectacularly-horned mountain goat. Building the Metro-alpin underground railway, at 11,482ft (3,500m) the highest train in the world, as an alternative to the difficult engineering problems of installing an above ground cableway, allows all year skiing on the Mittelallin glacier.

Among the many attractions are a new sports centre with tennis courts, sauna, swimming pool and solarium. Small bore rifle shooting, mini golf and guided walks are all available, in addition to instruction in high-level mountaineering and ski touring by the Saas-Fee mountaineering school.

Saas-Fee might be at the end of a cul-de-sac, but it is nevertheless a good centre for exploring the other high-level alpine villages of the Valais; Zermatt and the Matterhorn, for example, are just over the other side of the hill and can be reached easily by the Gornergrat railway by way of Brig and Visp.

Useful Information

Tourist Office
Verkersbüro
CH 3906 Saas-Fee
Telephone: 028 57 1457

Accommodation
From four-star hotels to bed and breakfast apartments. One campsite.

Cable cars
Plattjen	(gondola)
Felskinn	Mittelallin (cable car followed by Metro-Alpin underground railway).
Spielboden	Langflüe (gondola and cable car).
Hannig	(cable car).

Accessible Glaciers
Felskinn from the Felskinn cable car.
Mittelallin from the Metro-Alpin.
Fee from the Langflüe cable car.
Hohbalm above the Hannig lift.

Rail Excursions
Brig is easily accessible from Saas-Fee either by car or postbus and is an important rail centre with full or part day excursions to all points of southern Switzerland and northern Italy.

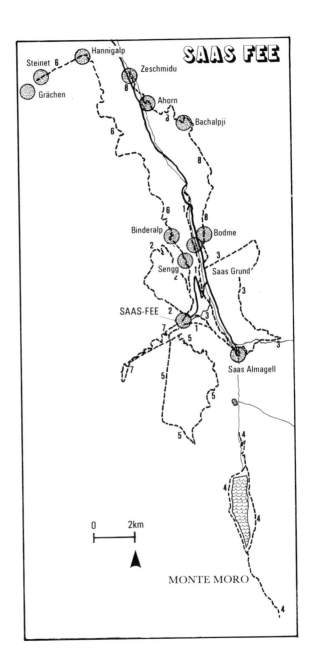

SAAS FEE

Steinet 6
Hannigalp
Grächen
Zeschmidu
Ahorn
Bachalpji
Binderalp
Bodme
Sengg
Saas Grund
SAAS-FEE
Saas Almagell

0   2km

MONTE MORO

153

THE SAAS VILLAGES — A VALLEY WALK

8¼ miles (13½km), 3-4 hours. Easy.

When visiting an area for the first time, no matter how much research has gone into preparing the holiday, and no matter how glowing the guidebooks are in their descriptions of the area, there is nothing to replace that first exciting exploratory walk. Here is such a walk; it visits all the little villages of the Upper Saaser Valley and gives us the opportunity of becoming quickly acquainted with the mountain scenery and architecture of the district. Weathered timber chalets and farmhouses compete with the icy peaks of this mountaineering centre. Dizzy heights of mountains on either hand range from the domed Allalinhorn to the rocky summits of the Mischabel group, whose highest summit, the Dom — 14,941ft (4,545m) — is easily recognised by its forked peak. The massive Fee glacier tumbles in frozen cascades above Saas-Fee, divided into two tongues by the Langflüe promontory.

Easy walking by the side of an alpine river links the valley hamlets of Saas Almagell, Saas Grund and Saas Balen.

The Route

□ Leave the centre of Saas-Fee and walk south past the indoor swimming pool towards the river and the keep fit course. Cross the river and follow a minor road, slightly uphill.

□ Turn left opposite the Pineta Gasthof and follow the footpath signposted to Saas Almagell.

□ Climb gently uphill into pine forest. Occasional rocky outcrops and old avalanche scars allow views across the valley and towards the village. Pines offer shade from the sun.

□ Continue along the forest track, gradually swinging around the lower shoulder of the Plattjen — 8,435ft (2,570m).

A signpost on the left points across a clearing to Bodme where there is a small farmhouse which sells refreshments.

□ Ignoring paths to the left and right of the track, walk down to Saas Almagell in the lower main valley.

There is an attractive view of Saas Almagell as you leave the confines of the forest about ¼ mile (400m) above the village. This is a relatively unaltered village, a community of farms in the upper valley.

□ After exploring Saas Almagell, retrace your steps as far as the river. Cross the bridge and turn right, downstream, to follow a path which roughly parallels the river. Crossing meadowland and through sparse forest, it skirts the attractive farm buildings of Alpji and then climbs slightly to avoid a narrow part of the valley.

After crossing meadows by Biele Farm, the path descends by a couple of zigzags into the pines and so rejoins the riverbank.

□ Turn left along the riverside and follow it away from the trees and across a series of fields to Unter den Bodmen.

□ Go through the hamlet by farm track towards and then over the Feevispa river.

The rough area, especially that above the north bank of the Feevispa, is moraine deposited by the Fee Glacier. Note how far the glacier has retreated from this spot; probably no more than two or three centuries have elapsed since it filled the whole of the upper Saas-Fee valley.

Fifteen small chapels mark a pilgrimage route from Saas-Fee through the rocks of the Hohen Stiege ('the high stairway') a little way above the valley path. Their attractive setting makes them well worth a visit.

□ Following the Feevispa, walk north through scrub pine and across rough pasture to the junction with the main river.

□ Continue along the riverbank and turn right to cross over to Saas Grund.

Saas Grund has a number of restaurants and gasthofs, and should make a convenient lunch stop.

□ Leave Saas Grund by recrossing the bridge; turn right and continue downstream, following the river's left bank.

□ Opposite Tamatten village, the path leaves the river, bearing left to cross a series of meadows to reach Bidermatten.

□ Climb gradually away from the village, through a belt of pines as far as three evenly-spaced streams. Cross these and start to walk downhill to the right, across stony ground. Enter an area of mature woodland.

□ Rejoin the river and follow it all the way to Saas Balen.

□ Return to Saas-Fee by local bus service.

The footpath enters Saas Balen by a curiously shaped round church with a narrow tower topped by the traditional 'onion' dome.

---

6 miles (9.6km), 3½ hours. Moderate/strenuous — 1,359ft
(414m) ascent.

The Hannig gondola lift takes most of the hard work out of the
3,164ft (964m) difference in height between Saas-Fee and the
summit of Mällig, leaving only a moderate climb above the top
station to the mountain crest.

An observant and silent walker should be rewarded with
glimpses of marmots, chamois and even the rare ibex. The walk
passes through three distinct zones of alpine flowers; around the
upper station of the Hannig lift, the ground is dotted with larger
plants such as anemones, and monkshood; higher, in rockier
regions, plants tend to be the cushion varieties or those delicate
flowers which can only bloom away from the competition of others,
in the shelter of rocks. Crocus and soldanella, probably the most
fragile of all alpines, bloom on the edge of snowfields, and in fact
soldanellas can often be found lifting their heads impatiently
through snow and even ice. Woodland flowers are different again,
and the observant walker will usually be able to see the smoky blue
of alpine clematis.

The Route

☐ Take the Hannig gondola lift to the top station and its restaurant.

☐ Follow the zigzag path uphill, away from the Saas-Fee side of the
restaurant.

*Try to come up as early as possible while the light is still clear, to
admire the breathtaking views of glaciers and mountains. The sun
terrace outside the Hannig restaurant must have one of the most
spectacular views in the area.*

☐ Climb gradually to the north-west, on a well-made path to the
first Mällig summit — 8,861ft (2,700m).

*A prominent rock formation about 1,000ft (305m) below and to the
north-west of the summit is known locally as the Chinese Wall, and is
probably a basalt dyke.*

☐ The angle of ascent eases, following the broad ridge round to the
main summit, at 9,071ft (2,764m).

☐ Turn right along the crest of the gently sloping north-east shoulder and follow the marked path for about ¾ mile (1.2km) downhill.

This is an excellent area for small alpine plants and also for wildlife such as marmots and chamois. Black alpine choughs will probably hover nearby whenever you stop for a snack. These masters of gliding are found around most alpine summits, especially where climbers and walkers stop for refreshment.

☐ The angle of descent increases slightly as the path leads first to the left, and then right through a zone of broken rock.

☐ Follow the zigzags as far as a footpath junction above the treeline.

☐ Turn right on a gently descending path through the mature pine forest of Balmiboden.

Look out for the alpine clematis and other woodland plants.

☐ At a fork take the right-hand path, slightly uphill, before beginning a steeper downhill section to the south-east.

☐ Cross an open space within the forest, and at a junction of four paths on its far side, turn left.

☐ Re-enter the forest and walk downhill into the northern outskirts of Saas-Fee.

A tiny Alpine chapel near Saas-Fee

3   THE SLOPES OF THE TRIFTHORN AND
ALMAGELLERALP

---

8 miles (13km), 4-5 hours. Easy/moderate.

Conveniently-sited cable cars around Saas-Fee have taken all the effort out of climbing above the main villages; with their help, the intermediate slopes and ridges have been opened up to all who wish to walk and climb in these remote regions.

From Im Grund in the lower valley, a gondola lift whisks the walker up to the Chrizbode top station, where a track, practically level for most of its length, swings round the lower slopes of the Trifthorn, barely losing 300ft (91m) in three miles (4.8km). In fact the total difference in height between Chrizbode and the Stafel farmhouse gasthof at Almagelleralp, almost at the end of the walk, is only 666ft (203m), but there are one or two slight ups and downs along the way!

As the day extends, the last leg of the walk is downhill through shady forest back to Saas-Fee, coming as a welcome relief on a hot day.

The Route

☐ Take the gondola lift to Chrizbode from the lower station at Im Grund, about half-way between Saas Grund and Unter dem Berg.

☐ Walk away from the upper station, slightly uphill, for about 50yd (46m) and turn right along a well-marked path, signposted to Almagelleralp.

☐ Climb gradually through a boulderfield crossing meltwater streams flowing from glaciers beneath Weissmies, 13,203ft (4,023m).

The rocky waste on either side of the path has been scoured from the west face of Weissmies by the Trift and Mällig glaciers.

☐ Beyond the moraine, the path follows a level course for about 2½ miles (4km).

The level path makes it easy to keep your eyes on the splendour of snow and ice covered peaks towering above Saas-Fee on the opposite side of the valley. However, bear in mind that the path is rocky in places and a simple slip could mean a sprained or broken ankle.

☐ Where the village of Saas Almagell comes into view in the valley below, the track climbs above a series of crags between the

Weissflue and Wäng hillsides.

☐ Start to walk downhill in a series of easy zigzags.

The ancient farmstead of Stafel on Almagelleralp sells light refreshments.

☐ Turn right beneath the service cable to Stafel and walk down the Almageller valley.

☐ The path loses height in a series of sweeping bends, and enters an area of rough woodland gradually improving all the way down to Saas Almagell.

☐ At a footpath junction above Saas Almagell, turn right and walk downhill to the road. Turn left into the village.

The postbus can be used to shorten the walk at this point if so desired.

☐ Walk into the centre of the village and turn right over the river.

☐ Take the second track, on the right beyond the bridge, and climb in a north-westerly direction, beneath mature pines.

☐ Turn right at the Bodme clearing (gasthof/refreshments).

☐ Take the left fork away from Bodme, downhill through pine trees and over the river.

☐ Climb through rough moraine on the far bank.

☐ Turn left on to the Hohen Stiege path to reach Saas-Fee.

Alpine barns above Saas-Fee

4 MATTMARK RESERVOIR AND THE SWISS-
ITALIAN FRONTIER (MONTE MORO PASS)

---

12 miles (19km), 5-6 hours. Moderate/strenuous — 2,182ft
(665m) ascent and descent.

Quite often alpine walks must be one-way affairs, and this is typical
of walks in high regions, where one must either descend to another
valley (and another country in this case), or more sensibly return by
more or less the same route. The walk is in no way inferior as a
result; views up and down a valley are always different and
therefore one can make interesting comparisons. The main
advantage of this walk is that it leads to the high alpine pass of
Monte Moro — 9,413ft (2,868m) — which marks one of the 'nicks'
in the mountain chain separating Switzerland from Italy.

Just across the summit of the pass there is an Italian Mountaineering
Club hut, the Rifugio Città di Malnate, which makes a welcome
feature at the high point of the walk. In case of emergencies, such as
sudden bad weather, there is a cable way down from the hut to the
village of Macugnaga.

As this walk is into a high mountainous region, especially on a
north-facing ridge, there is every possibility of snow lingering well
into the summer. If you come to a steep snowfield barring the way
and conditions are perhaps a little icy, it is safest to turn back unless
all your party have ice axes and can use them. In any case, it will be
wise to check on conditions beforehand, by asking at the local
tourist office.

The Route

□ The walk starts at the foot of the Mattmark Reservoir. It should
be possible to park a car nearby or reach it by postbus, but check
locally beforehand.

□ Climb to the dam by its access road, and walk towards the east
shore of the reservoir.

*The view along the lake is towards the peaks and connecting ridges
which mark the Swiss-Italian frontier. Monte Moro – 9,793ft
(2,984m) – is directly ahead, and the notch of the pass, the objective of
the walk, is a little to its left around its eastern shoulder.*

☐ Follow the east shore and then climb above a rocky area.

☐ Cross a side valley, the Ofental, and rejoin the reservoir at its southern end.

At the head of the reservoir, high alpine pasture is grazed by animals which spend the short summer months in meadows close by the farms near Wäng.

☐ Follow a waymarked track through the debris of ancient glaciers, gradually gaining height all the time.

☐ Keep to the waymarked route and cross small streams created by meltwaters from nearby glaciers.

☐ At the summit of the pass, pause to admire the view and then swing round to the right beneath the Monte Moro to reach the Italian Alpine Club hut, the Rifugio Città di Malnate.

The view from the pass is just reward for the climb; the massif of Monte Rosa stands proudly to the south-west, on your right, with the Dufourspitze, 15,209ft (4,634m), Switzerland's highest point, as it's main summit. Macugnaga village is below, in Italy, at the head of the Val d'Anzasca which eventually drains into Lake Maggiore.

☐ Retrace your steps downhill as far as the alpine farms at the head of the reservoir.

☐ Turn left and follow a level track above the west bank of the reservoir as far as the dam wall.

☐ Walk down the road from the dam to reach the car park.

5 A GLACIER WALK AND AROUND THE
MITTAGHORN

$4\frac{1}{2}$ miles (7km), returning to the Felskinn top station of the
Plattjen lift, $2\frac{1}{2}$ hours. Optional extension of $2\frac{1}{2}$ miles (4km) and
2,432ft (741m) descent to Saas-Fee, 4 hours.
Moderate/strenuous.

**Check locally about conditions on the glaciers around the Britannia
hut and also of the path from the hut to Plattjen, before starting on
this exceptional high-level walk.**

Pick your day for this walk, which could be the highlight of a
holiday in the Saas-Fee area. Here is a safe high-level glacier walk to
a mountain hut, followed by a path through a rocky wilderness. On
this walk, a newcomer to alpine walking can experience at first hand
the awesome feeling of being at one with nature.

This is a walk to spend all day over, and with the Plattjen lift at the
end, it is possible to remain at high-level for as long as you like and
then return in comfort.

There is, for those with time and energy, a choice of routes back
down the forested slopes to Saas-Fee.

The Route

□ Take the Plattjen cable car to its upper station at Felskinn, 9,816ft
(2,991m).

*As an option the Metro-alpin, the world's highest underground
railway can be used. It runs from Felskinn to Mittelallin – 11,342ft
(3,456m), to emerge in the centre of a glacial wilderness. There is also
an ice grotto, and other attractions, near the Felskinn terminus.*

□ Follow the signposted path from behind the Felskinn station out
on to the Chessjen glacier.

□ Climb to the south-east, across the snow-covered glacier as far as
the low col at Egginerjoch.

*Look back from below the col to the massive cirque of peaks and
glaciers surrounding Saas-Fee.*

□ Follow a more-or-less level course over the glacier and beneath
the Hinter Allalin ridge to the Britannia Hut.

The Britannia Hut is one of the many alpine refuges owned by the

Swiss Alpine Club. The hut provides refreshments and accommodation to members and non-members alike, but the former get special terms. However, no-one would ever be turned away from a hut in unfavourable weather, or if they were tired or ill.

▢ Leave the hut by the marked track, a little west of north, and drop gently down to a small glacial lake.

The lake and its stony surrounds are typical of the environment around the foot of a gently sloping glacier.

▢ Climb away from the lake across boulder-strewn, glacier-worn slabs.

Look out for small alpine plants in sunny pockets throughout this part of the walk.

▢ Ignore a footpath descending steeply on the right, but walk ahead on a level course through the boulderfield.

▢ Start to lose height and swing round the eastern shoulder of the rocky Mittaghorn — 10,315ft (3,143m).

The view south is towards the Moro Pass, and north along the main Saas valley.

▢ Around the shoulder of the Mittaghorn, the way is level almost until the Plattjen upper station comes into view. Walk by easy zigzags down to the station.

A decision must be made at this point, either to use the gondola lift or to walk all the way back to Saas-Fee. If the latter, then the following route is recommended.

▢ Walk downhill beneath the cable and turn left at a path junction.

▢ The path zigzags down the steep rocky hillside as far as the treeline. Ignore paths off to the right and left, below the main forest area.

▢ Pass a remote farmstead and follow the sweeping zigzags in and out of a deforested zone.

▢ Go right and then left at a junction with a level path.

▢ Join a rough road and turn right to pass the lower Plattjen cable station.

▢ Walk back to Saas-Fee by way of Zum Steg.

6

GRÄCHEN TO SAAS-FEE
(THE BALFRIN HIGH-LEVEL TRAIL)

---

10 miles (16km), 6½ hours. Strenuous.

The walk starts at Grächen on the far side of the mountains from Saas-Fee, and to get there it will be necessary either to use the postbus out from Saas-Fee via Stalden, or to drive there; leave the car and return by postbus on completion of the walk. Check times beforehand.

An advantage of the walk is that it visits a new village and a walking area in a valley near, yet so different, away from the 'home based' mountains. Grächen is a pleasant little place; road access is by a steep side road from the Mittertal valley, the route to Zermatt and the Matterhorn. Grächen has the usual attractions expected of an alpine village; shops, gasthofs, an attractive old church and, more important, a cableway which takes the effort out of the initial climb up to the beginning of the walk.

The route followed by this walk is along the well-defined track of the Balfrin high-level trail. It is easy to follow, even though it has sections over rocky ground and can be a little exposed in places. This is a long walk, but one which, if given sufficient time, can prove to be an enjoyable experience. With only minor exceptions, the route is above the treeline until almost within sight of Saas-Fee.

The Route

□ Use the cableway from Grächen to reach Hannigalp.

□ Follow the signposted Balfrinalp path to the right, starting at the side of a small building about 100yd (91m) north-east of the upper station.

□ Climb through an area of stunted pines and head south-east.

□ Keep left at a footpath junction. The climbing eases and the path follows a level contour-hugging route over rocky ground to lonely Balfrinalp.

Sunny, south-facing areas should make excellent hunting grounds for alpine flower lovers. Marmots and possibly chamois are likely to be seen by those who are quiet enough, when passing beneath the slopes of Stock – 8,175ft (2,491m).

☐ Bear right at a path junction on the far side of Balfrinalp, and walk downhill to the headwaters of the Schweibbach river.

☐ Cross the stream and follow a level path around the rocky lower slopes of the Lammenhorn — 10,466ft (3,189m).

☐ The path now begins to descend gradually. Ignore paths off to the side until the dark masses of the Biderwald forest are reached.

☐ Walk on into the forest, downhill, as far as a path junction at the head of a little dry valley.

☐ Keep right, slightly uphill, then go down into the clearing of Egge.

☐ Left at a path junction, back into the shade of the pine forest on an improving forest track which leads directly into the eastern outskirts of Saas-Fee.

Check locally for times of the postbus to Grächen; it may be necessary to leave the car overnight, and perhaps its collection could be linked to an excursion to Zermatt.

Saas-Fee

7   SAAS-FEE AND ITS LAKE FROM THE
LANGFLÜE CABLE CAR

4½ miles (7km), 2-3 hours. Easy/moderate — 3,558ft (1,084m)
descent.

Of all the cable lifts in the Saas-Fee area, the dual system which
takes the visitor with such ease to the top of the Langflüe ridge is
unquestionably the most dramatic. The ridge acts as a sort of
breakwater, or more correctly ice-breaker, and divides the
awesome cascades of the lower and final stages of the Fee glacier.
To use the descriptive breakwater simile again, the icefalls look like
gigantic surf, which has been frozen in the act of crashing on to a
rocky beach; the beach in this case being the Saas valley.

This walk is all downhill, but nonetheless a downhill walk on
which the pedestrian will want to linger. It follows a carefully-
planned path which loses height with a multitude of sinuous twists
and turns down the Langflüe ridge as far as Gletscheralp.

At the foot of the ridge, and where the two arms of the glacier
once met, there is a moraine lake which is a startling emerald
colour.

The Route

□ Take the cable car first to Spielboden, and then to the top of
Langflüe.

□ Walk uphill away from the top station and swing round to the
opposite side of the Langflüe's spur.

□ Go downhill on a well-marked path across broken ground to the
top station of the Spielboden lift.

□ Follow the zigzag path downhill.

□ At a junction of about six routes, take the far left and swing round,
first above it for the best views, and then down to the emerald-green
moraine lake.

□ Take the lower of three left-turning paths away from the lake, and
walk through a short stretch of pine forest.

□ Turn right on reaching the far side of the forest.

□ Left and join the main path back through flat meadowland in to
Saas-Fee.

7 miles (11.25km), $3\frac{1}{2}$ hours. Moderate.

In many of the more attractive resorts, it is useful to know of a walk where an escape from the crowded sections of more popular routes can be almost guaranteed. This is just such a walk. It starts from Unter dem Berg and climbs gradually towards the summer farms of Bodme. It then goes through dense pine woods, in and out of man-made clearings, still farmed in summer by the descendants of the men who cut down the massive trees and hacked out their roots centuries ago. This was farming husbandry at its most primitive, but it remains a method which is employed throughout the forested world even today.

Above Saas Balen the path crosses a rough open area, the partly-overgrown one-time terminal moraine of a glacier, which has now shrunk to a fraction of its original shape and size beneath the upper slopes of the Fletschhorn.

A gently rising track leads around the western slopes of the Rothorn before crossing the Mattwaldbach stream, and then descending partly through forest, to a road near the tiny farming settlement of Ahorn.

It will be necessary, before starting out on this walk, to find the times of the postbuses back from Ahorn, otherwise a taxi will be required to avoid a tiring road walk to Saas-Fee.

The Route

☐ Take the morning postbus or drive to Unter dem Berg. The walk starts from the centre of the village away from the main road.

☐ Climb uphill, away from the houses, and aim towards the Triftbach stream.

☐ Turn left over the stream and then immediately fork right on a footpath which climbs steadily uphill through a pine wood interspersed with small natural clearings.

☐ Pass a small calvary shrine and climb, fairly steeply, by zigzags to the chapel of St Joseph.

The chapel, in its lonely situation, is typical of those found in alpine regions. The view alone is a justification for building the chapel here.

☐ Fork left at the chapel, and climb along the upper edge of a mature forest, to the Bodme farms.

◻ Walk north, away from Bodme into dense pine forest.

◻ Skirt the upper edge of a clearing around the Trewaldji farmsteads.

It is usually possible to buy milk, and maybe light refreshments, at most of the farms passed along the way.

◻ Still climbing, re-enter the forest and walk beneath pines until the Brend clearing is reached.

◻ Cross the rough open moraine-filled area on either side of the Fell stream.

Moraine tends to attract certain types of plants. All have long root systems to reach down to the plentiful supply of water beneath the underlying gravel.

◻ Beyond a group of small farm buildings and a tiny chapel, turn right and then almost immediately left. Cross a boulder field and then follow a path above an outcropping crag.

◻ Go left at a path junction to aim north-west along the upper limits of a mature pine forest.

◻ Climb by a gently rising path, around the western slopes of the Rothorn — 10,341ft (3,151m).

The flat-topped alp at point 2244, below the Rotgufer moraine, makes an ideal resting place or picnic stop. The views across the valley are quite sublime.

◻ Cross a wild region of rocks and scree, the remnants of an old moraine, and walk down to the Mattwaldbach river. Take care when crossing the stream, especially if it is in spate in late spring.

◻ Beyond the river, the path forks. Take the left path and begin to descend.

◻ Follow a system of bends of the cleverly-designed path, down through forest to the clearing of Zer Matte. Continue downnill on rocky ground as far as Ahorn.

◻ Go through the settlement and follow the jeep track as far as the main road, which is joined by the side of a tunnel entrance. If you are not relying on the postbus it will be necessary to walk about ½ mile (800m) further along the road to Ze Schmidu village for a public telephone, and also for refreshments.

APPENZELL

Maps

Landeskarte der Schweiz (1:50,000 Series). Sheet 227 — Appenzell
or Sheet 5014 — St Gallen; Appenzell.

How to get there:

Road:

1   Via the Black Forest and Schaffhausen to Lake Constance
(Bodensee) and St Gallen. South-west by minor road to Appenzell.
2   European motorway network to Basel. East to Zürich and St
Gallen, then south-west.

Rail:

Main line to St Gallen via Zürich, then branch line (narrow gauge)
to Appenzell.

Air:

International airports at Basel and Zürich with rail connections
above.

The Area

The locally-produced guide advises that this is a centre for homely
holidays, and for once a publicity statement is correct. If there can
be any critism of this description, understatement is the only word
which comes to mind. Here, in this north-east corner of Switzerland,
tucked between the heights of the Säntis mountain in the south-
west and Lake Constance to the north, is a tranquil region which
manages to cater for tourists and yet remains completely unspoilt
by the trappings of tourism.

Fertile valleys have been husbanded for centuries and dairy
farming is the major industry. The local cheese is ideal for grilling,
and is usually offered toasted as *raclette* in the cafes and

restaurants, of the tiny towns and villages. Cows are still much valued; the animals are decked with flowers and hung with massive bells for their annual migrations to and from the high pastures. The privilege of carrying the heaviest bell goes to the lead cow, a position which is often keenly fought over in the herd.

Cowbell-ringing and *Talerschwingen* are local customs, and while bell-ringing may be heard in concerts, as often as not a group of villagers will set up an impromptu recital in a friendly bar. *Talerschwingen* is the bell-like sound made by swinging a five franc piece (a *taler*) inside a large earthenware bowl; usually a late-night rendering after a convivial evening!

This is a region of old buildings as well as customs. Many of the fine structures date from the sixteenth century; the town hall in particular is well worth a visit. Inside, there is a museum of folklore where some of the locally-worked lace is on display.

Appenzell canton is a self-governing region where the Landesgemeinde, or open-air parliament, is still held. Local men vote on issues requiring a simple 'Yes' or 'No' by holding a sword aloft.

Many of the high valleys hold jewel-like lakes, and most are easy to reach. Postbuses and the tiny electric railway make every valley accessible to the adventurous walker.

Walking can be as varied as anyone would wish, from wandering along cool forest tracks, or exploring tiny villages, to the easy ridge walking of Hoher Kasten or Ebenalp, both easily accessible by the use of cable cars.

While the Säntis peak dominates the south-western edge of this region and its summit may be reached by a cable car above Schwägalp, it is perhaps the more lowly Hoher Kasten which will offer a better reward for the walker. The mountain is made from carboniferous limestone, layers of which have been contorted into huge folds by primeval earth movements. The ridge walk has views of the Rhine valley in the east and the beautiful Brüel valley to the west.

Useful Information

Tourist Office
Verkehrsbüro
CH 9043 Trogen
Telephone: 071 94 13 16

Accommodation
Homely hotels, guest houses, rented apartments and campsites.

Cable Cars and Chair Lifts

Wasserauen   — Ebenalp (chairlift)
Brülisau   — Hoher Kasten (cable car)
Schwägalp   — Säntis (cable car)
Jakobsbad   — Kronberg (cable car)

Steam Railway

Toggenburgbahn — twelve miles of track from Herisau to Nesslau in the Thur valley. Standard gauge, privately-owned line, popular with wedding parties.

Lake Cruises

Lake Constance (Bodensee). Regular cruises and ferry service to and from Rorschach. Note: carry passports and currency if leaving the ferry at one of the Austrian or German resorts.

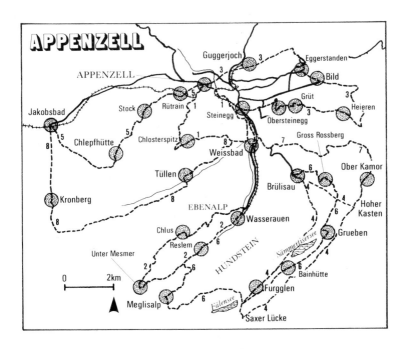

1

APPENZELL TOWN, WEISSBAD AND THE CHLOSTERSPITZ

7¼ miles (11.6km), 4 hours. Easy/moderate — 1,085ft (330m) ascent.

This walk is a good introduction to the area around Appenzell. It is an obvious first-day walk which threads its way through the old town and allows time to discover the layout and find where the best shops are. On the latter point, Appenzell has an excellent selection of bakers' shops as well as greengrocers and butchers, and time spent in the early morning buying in supplies for the day's picnic can be one of the highlights of a holiday. Remember that shops open early in Switzerland and unless you are making an alpine start, ie before dawn, it pays to buy fresh each day.

After a gentle stroll along the river, with a convenient coffee stop at Weissbad, the route climbs the wooded slopes of the Chlosterspitz — 4,348ft (1,325m), where clearings in the forest look out over views of the surrounding countryside. Below Chlosterspitz, an easy track leads downhill across the alpine pastures of its lower slopes.

Appenzell is re-entered from the opposite direction to that taken at the start of the walk, completing the opportunity of exploring this ancient town. Anyone visiting the area in either spring or autumn should be able to see the spectacle of decorated cows, some carrying massive bells, being led to or from their summer grazing.

The Route

□ Walk through the old town as far as the bridge.

Look out for the Rathaus (town hall) and ornate shop buildings in the main street.

□ Cross the River Sitter and turn right to follow a riverside path as far as the railway crossing at Sittertal. Join the road which runs parallel to the railway line. Do not cross the river.

□ Still following the river upstream, walk along the road for about 180yd (165m), and turn right where the road leaves the riverbank.

□ Follow the riverside path through a belt of trees and rejoin the road.

□ Continue, by road, to Weissbad. This should be convenient for an early coffee stop.

□ Turn right through Weissbad and cross the river.

□ Three tracks divide on the far side of the bridge; take the far left and climb through meadowland to the farm of Rechböhl.

□ Go left on the minor road beyond the farm and then take the second right which is a forest access track.

□ Leave the track after about 100yd (91m), and follow the signposted path steeply uphill through mature pine forest. Climb slowly on to the east ridge of the Chlosterspitz.

□ The angle eases at the clearing and meadowland around Chlispitz farm.

□ Walk through the forest again until the summit clearing is reached.

There are good views of the Säntis – 8,215ft (2,503m) – from the top of the Chlosterspitz.

□ Start to walk downhill towards farm buildings at Neuenalp, lower down the ridge.

□ Turn right, away from the farm and along its access track. Go straight on where another track joins it from the left.

□ Take the right fork by the upper station of a service lift.

□ Follow the cable downhill across open pasture for about ¼ mile (400m) and swing left towards a belt of pine trees. Continue downhill into the modern part of Appenzell and aim for the railway station. The town centre is about 150yd (137m) further on.

6½ miles (10.4km), 4 hours. Moderate/strenuous.

This walk is preceded by a train ride. The narrow gauge railway which wanders all round the region has a branch line from Appenzell as far as Wasserauen. A cable car from here lifts walkers with consummate ease almost to the summit of Ebenalp at 5,382ft (1,640m).

Before continuing the walk along the ridge from Ebenalp to Schäfler, walk through a short tunnel to the little chapel of Wildkirchli. The chapel sits on a narrow ledge high above the Schwendibach valley, and excavations have revealed that this is the site of one of the the oldest prehistoric settlements in Switzerland.

The ridge to Schäfler — 6,311ft(1,923m), is narrow in places, but this exciting little scramble is well within the capabilities of anyone experienced in hillwalking, providing they have a good head for heights, are wearing boots with properly patterned soles, and the weather is good.

To the west of Schäfler, the path which at first follows the ridge, veers off, downhill to the left of Altenalptürm — 6,666ft (2,031m), and drops steeply towards the high alpine tarm of Unter Mesmer. The track turns left and the angle of descent eases out on to meadows above the Seealpsee lake. From here an easy track leads back along a wooded ravine to Wasserauen.

The Route

□ Use the cable car from Wasserauen to reach Ebenalp.

□ After visiting the summit, walk downhill past the restaurant and follow the signposted path to the Wildkirchli tunnel.

The chapel, perched on its ledge, makes a fine viewpoint across the nearby ridges towards the Hoher Kasten limestone ridge.

□ Follow the safe but exposed ledge away from the church.

□ Keep right at two footpath junctions and gradually climb up to the west ridge of Ebenalp.

□ Regain the ridge at the little group of buildings on an exploded alp at Chlus.

□ Turn left and climb along the rocky ridge to the summit of Schäfler.

☐ Continue along its west ridge, downhill to a path junction on the south-east slopes of Altenalptürm.

☐ Turn left, and almost immediately right, to point 1754 on the Lötzlisalpsattel spur.

☐ Bear left, steeply downhill, across the rocky hillside to a group of summer farms at Unter Mesmer.

Säntis – 8,215ft (2,503m), towers above the valley head to the south-west of the Mesmer alp; there is usually a patch of snow, the Blau Schnee, lying beneath the summit ridge throughout the summer months.

☐ Turn left away from the farm buildings, at first steeply over rocky ground, but gradually at an easier angle where the grazing of the Seealp is reached.

☐ Pass a number of farms and timber barns to reach the Seealpsee.

The Seealpsee makes an attractive foreground to photographic studies of Säntis which, if conditions are right, can be seen mirrored in the lake.

☐ Follow the valley track, through the narrow wooded gorge of the upper Schwendibach river, all the way back to Wasserauen.

Typical Appenzell scenery with Säntis in the background

175

3   HIRSCHBERG AND FORSTSEELI LAKE
(A FOREST AND MEADOW WALK)

12 miles (19.3km), 6-7 hours. Moderate.

Even in Switzerland, which normally has an excellent summer climate, one can still encounter rain. This walk is therefore recommended for those days when, for one reason or another, a high-level route is impossible.

Basically, the walk climbs the Hirschberg ridge before crossing the broad col between the Aubach valley and a small side valley which flows down to Appenzell. Forest tracks lead across the Bildstein area to the tiny lake of Forstseeli — 3,922ft (1,195m). On the return, the route contours across the middle slopes of the Fänerenspitz — 4,943ft (1,506m), to reach the gasthof at Eggli. From here an easy track leads downhill to the village of Steinegg and a pleasant riverside stroll finishes the last leg of the walk back to Appenzell.

Careful route finding is necessary amongst the complicated footpath system near the Forstseeli lake, but on no account should this gem be omitted from the walk.

Sheltered meadows, especially those on the high section of the walk, are full of wildflowers in early summer. Even though they will be scythed down at haymaking, they still return year after year, a telling record of the success of the practice of manuring pasture without the use of chemical fertilisers. This tried and true method has been employed for countless generations and as a result, once-poor, rocky soil has become lush and fertile, producing rich milk yields from the special breed of cattle suited to this environment.

The Route

□ Cross the bridge away from the main street in Appenzell and walk in a north-easterly direction along the road towards the bypass.

□ Cross the bypass with care, and take the righthand of two farm lanes.

□ Walk uphill, past a group of buildings lining the road to reach another road, this time running parallel to the railway line.

□ Turn left along the road for about 100yd (91m) and then right to cross the railway.

□ Follow a farm track to the Guggerloch.

□ Keep ahead at a path crossing, and follow the signposted and waymarked path up the easy slopes of the Hirschberg ridge.
Good views back towards Appenzell and the Sitter valley.

□ At point 1052, turn right downhill, over improving meadowland in a break between two sections of pine forest.

□ Beyond Weier, turn right on a local road and then left at the road junction. Walk by road through the scattered hamlet of Eggerstanden to another road junction at Bild.

□ Turn left along the road past Bild church as far as point 910.

□ Fork right on to a minor forest road, the surface of which gradually deteriorates into a gravel track.

□ Follow the track in and out of belts of mature forest, through Bildstein, climbing gradually and aiming southwards.

□ Reach the pine-shrouded Forstseeli lake.

□ Turn right away from the lake in a north-westerly direction. ignore tracks to the right or left and cross a small stream.

□ Leave the forest by a path contouring round the slopes of Fänerenspitz until a farm track is reached. Follow this, almost due west.

□ A footpath junction signals the proximity of the Eggli gasthof.

□ Follow the road away from Eggli down to Steinegg village.

□ Go through Steinegg and turn right, by road along the riverbank, as far as the road bridge.

□ Turn right, away from the bridge, to follow an easy path on the east bank of the river, all the way to Appenzell.

4   HOHER KASTEN RIDGE WALK

---

10 miles (16km), 6 hours. Moderate/strenuous — 2,386ft (727m) descent.

Aided by the cable car from the village of Brülisau (4 miles, 6.4km south-east of Appenzell), walkers can easily reach the narrow limestone ridge of the Hoher Kasten and then follow the well-made and clearly marked path to the south-west along its airy crest. A convenient mountain hut, about half-way along the ridge, makes an ideal stopping place at lunchtime. The high-level part of the walk finishes at the narrow col of Saxer Lücke. Steep tracks lead down to the lake of Sämtisersee with yet another well-sited refreshment stop. An easy road leads back to Brülisau.

The rocks which make up the Hoher Kasten ridge were formed in a tropical sea millions of years ago. The almost pure white carboniferous limestone is mostly made up of sea creatures and plants, living in an environment which contrasts sharply with the present day inland and elevated situation of Hoher Kasten. The ridge walk has been made all the more interesting by the placing of plaques at regular intervals, explaining, in German, the story of the rock formations seen along the ridge. It does not matter if technical German is beyond your linguistic ability, as easy-to-follow diagrams can be related to the surrounding rocks.

The Route

□ Either take the bus or park the car in Brülisau village and take the cable car to the top of Hoher Kasten — 5,891ft (1,795m), where there is a small restaurant for an early morning coffee.

□ Turn right, downhill, away from the restaurant and upper station to follow the well-made path in comfort along the narrow limestone ridge.

Keep a lookout for the prominently-displayed plaques which explain the story of the rocks.

□ The path keeps mainly to the crest, but where the ridge narrows it turns to the right of any potentially dangerous place.

The view to the south-east is across the Rhine valley; the river flows towards Lake Constance (Bodensee). On the far bank is the tiny principality of Liechtenstein; surprisingly, part of geographical

Austria despite its political links with Switzerland.

□ Ignore side tracks to the right or left and continue along the ridge.

At the foot of the stubby little hill of Stauberenchanzlen, which sticks up like a thumb from the main ridge, there is a small restaurant which will probably be welcomed as a chance for an early lunch.

□ Climb Stauberenchanzlen by the path which follows the easiest route, away from the restaurant and to the right of the rockiest part of the ridge.

□ Continue beneath the crest, first slightly uphill and then down to a narrow gap in the ridge. This is Saxer Lücke — 5,412ft (1,649m), and the end of the high-level part of the walk.

A family of marmots can often be seen near the col, but only if you approach quietly. Patriarchs of the clan sit as lookouts on top of the communal burrow and warn of approaching danger from either humans or birds of prey, by giving a high-pitched whistle.

□ Turn right at Saxer Lücke and walk steeply downhill over rocky ground to the alpine farm at Bollenmees.

□ Turn right at Bollenmees and follow a rough track past a small shrine and across alpine meadowland.

□ Keep left, still on the track, through the summer farmsteads of Furglenn. Walk gradually downhill through the forest of Rhodwald to the flat area above the Sämtisersee; climb above the lake, through forest to the pretty gasthof restaurant at Plattenbödeli.

□ Follow the roadway downhill away from Plattenbödeli, through the narrow wooded gorge of Brüeltobel out to the open fields above Brülisau.

□ A mile or so of road leads back to the village.

5 AN AFTERNOON'S WALK TO APPENZELL
FROM JAKOBSBAD

8 miles (5km), 4 hours. Easy — 1,324ft (483m) ascent.

Here is a pleasant way to spend an afternoon; it does not involve much climbing and the views from Scheidegg — 4,437ft (1,352m), at the highest point in the walk, are of the Säntis massif to the south.

The countryside through which this walk passes is a mixture of rolling flowery meadows and broad pine-clad ridges. The final mile looks down on Appenzell spread like a toy town beyond the railway. Farmland beyond the town limits is used to graze that placid breed of alpine cattle who produce milk destined to become Appenzell cheese. This, the local version of Gruyère made into almost cartwheel-sized rings, can be seen maturing in dairies dotted throughout the local countryside.

The Swiss still manage to run their little railways into the remotest valleys, and this walk can be combined with a short journey along one of them. The narrow-gauge train which runs from Appenzell to the Urnasch valley can be used to reach Jakobsbad and the start of the walk.

The Route

☐ Leave Jakobsbad railway station and follow the narrow lane south-east, away from the railway and also the lower station of the Kronberg cable car. The lane crosses farmland and passes several small farms.

☐ Keep straight on where a side track turns left for the Jakobsbad campsite.

☐ At a junction of the lane with two minor roads, turn left on the first road, then after about 100yd (91m), right on the second.

☐ Follow this road, uphill into pine forest, as far as a junction.

☐ Turn left at the junction and walk steadily uphill, still in forest, but on a gradually lessening gradient.

☐ The track moves out to open meadowland near the Nas farmstead. Follow signposts to Scheidegg.

☐ A little beyond the lower station of a service cable to Scheidegg, the ground steepens but the track climbs the hillside in a broad sweep, first to the left and then right, to reach a junction of tracks and footpaths in front of the Scheidegg gasthof restaurant.

Scheidegg is an obvious place to stop; to take a short rest, or have a meal, but certainly to enjoy the views south towards Säntis and east into the Vorarlberg mountains of Western Austria.

□ Retrace your footsteps a little way, to the north-east along the ridge, but turn right at the junction with the outward path.

□ Fork left between a couple of ridge top barns and walk downhill, skirting the lower edge of a small pine wood. Ignore a path to the right below the wood.

□ Below the wood, aim for the group of four buildings of Chlepfhütten farm. They sit on the end of a short turf-covered hillside spur.

□ Turn right, away from the farmhouse and down the broad grassy hillside. Walk as far as a wayside chapel at a crossing of four tracks.

□ Walk ahead with the chapel on the left, down into and then across a small wooded valley.

□ Cross an open meadow and then another wooded valley to reach a group of barns and small farms.

□ Join a minor road and follow it, slanting across the broad forested hillside.

□ Walk steadily downhill, over the railway and directly into the town centre of Appenzell.

*The path from
Hoher Kasten to
Fälensee*

$11\frac{1}{2}$ miles (18.5km), 7 hours. Strenuous — 3,065ft (934m) ascent.

This is a tough walk, but one which will give tremendous satisfaction; for not only does it visit three delightful lakes, but also covers a wide variety of alpine countryside. The walk begins in the rural atmosphere of Brülisau, and crosses alpine meadows beneath the soaring limestone crags of the Hoher Kasten; meadows which have been created by centuries of careful husbandry and which are, in early summer, a colourful blaze of every imaginable alpine flower. The first lake, Sämtisersee, is glimpsed through breaks in the pine-clad slopes; the path skirts then the eastern end of Fälensee, filling a narrow cleft between the Hundstein and Roslenfirst. The hardest part of the walk is between Fälensee and Seealpsee, but this last of the three lakes comes as just reward almost at the end of a hard day's walk. From Seealpsee an easy track leads to the road at Wasserauen where there is the choice of either train or bus back to Appenzell.

As the starting and finishing points of this walk are not the same, it is necessary to check local bus and rail timetables beforehand. The service, however, is excellent and there should be no problem linking with the schedule.

The Route

☐ Take the service bus to Brülisau. Turn left, away from the village square, and walk up the road past the church which should then be on the left.

☐ At a junction of tracks, turn right to follow the footpath signposted to the Sämtisersee. Climb steadily over the grassy lower slopes of the Hoher Kasten ridge.

☐ Ignore side paths on the left, and follow the main path, which swings right beneath the Hoher Kasten cable car route. Follow a gently climbing course, and continue through sparse pine woods and pasture almost to Sämtisersee.

☐ Turn left at the junction with the Plattenbödeli path (the restaurant is only about $\frac{1}{2}$ mile (800m) away, if an early refreshment stop is desired).

☐ Turn right at the group of farm buildings of Grueben.

☐ Climb steadily through forest, above Sämtisersee lake.

Even though the path does not actually visit the lake, the side views through clearings in the Rhodwald pine forest are delightful.

☐ Ignoring side tracks, walk on towards Bollenmees and Fälensee.

Bollenmees restaurant will come as a welcome break after the climb through Rhodwald; its balcony looks out on a view along Fälensee, and makes an ideal refreshment stop.

☐ Follow the path north from Bollenmees along the forest edge, with rocky lower slopes of the Hundstein — 7,076ft (2,156m), on the left.

☐ Turn left for the signposted path to Meglisalp.

This is the hardest section of the walk; the path climbs steeply over rocky slopes and sparse pasture to reach the settlement of Widderalp. Beyond, the path is stony and needs care, both uphill and down to Meglisalp.

☐ Turn right at a group of barns and walk down to the sheltered hollow of Meglisalp, where refreshments can be bought at one of the farms.

Meglisalp is a surprisingly level alp, which sits at the top of a complex system of hanging valleys. Access is so steep that goods and even young animals are carried up by a small private cable lift.

☐ Follow the signposted path, north-east and downhill to Seealpsee. The path soon leaves the easy ground of Meglisalp, taking a slanting course down the rocky slopes of Schrenen and then into forest through breaks in its lower crags to the lakeside.

Take exceptional care on this last steep rocky section of the walk, as it would be a pity to mar such a memorable expedition with an accident in the last stage.

☐ There is a choice of routes around the shores of Seealpsee, and there is a farmhouse restaurant at its northern corner.

☐ Climb a little, uphill, away from the lake, then downhill along the signposted track alongside the Schwendibach stream to Wasserauen and the end of the walk.

7 miles (11.2km), 4 hours. Easy/moderate.

Even for those following these walks in the order in which they are listed, and who have already been up Hoher Kasten, this walk should still have an appeal. Not only does it offer the opportunity to visit the limestone peak for a second time, but it also completes the exploration of the mountain by following the line of its north-eastern ridge.

Another advantage of the walk is that the north-east ridge is not visited by many people; most visitors confine themselves to the south-western aspect. As a result, no matter how crowded the summit may be, this walk is likely to be very quiet for most of the day.

The route climbs through a high combe overlooking the Rhine valley, before traversing open meadows and across forested slopes, and descending gradually to the main valley. Weissbad and its interesting architecture marks the start of the easy riverside stroll all the way back to Appenzell.

The Route

☐ Take the cable car from Brülisau to the top of Hoher Kasten.

☐ Turn left, to the north-east, away from the upper station, and walk downhill around the grassy Chüestein shoulder.

☐ Cross the rocky upper section of the combe and walk as far as the group of buildings on the high alp of Ober Kamor.

The River Rhine, far beneath the steep eastern wall of Hoher Kasten, is almost canal-like and has been tamed to prevent flooding. The flat fertile valley bottom has some of the richest agricultural land in Switzerland.

☐ Follow a farm track over a slight rise, then down to more farms at Unter Kamor.

☐ Walk to the west of a little hill and on to the broad col of Resspass.

☐ Turn left, downhill, through a small pine forest.

☐ At a crossing of tracks turn left on a forest road. Follow signs for Weissbad.

☐ Keep to the right at other junctions until a track crossing is reached by the side of a small stream.

□ Walk ahead at the crossing, downhill through farmland, passing a small wayside shrine on the left.

□ The track, improving as its descends, joins the main valley road by the side of a road bridge.

□ Turn right along the road for about ½ mile (800m), then left across the railway and into Weissbad.

The distintive style of buildings in Weissbad are typical of the architecture of the Appenzell district. This is a rainy area, and farm buildings tend to be grouped in a single unit with the animals and domestic accommodation all under one wooden shingled roof. Cellars have windows at ground level making a workroom of even temperature.

□ Walk through the village, cross both the Schwendibach and Weissbach river, turning right on to the water meadows by the side of the latter.

□ Walk along the riverbank, below Steinegg and Sittertal all the way to Appenzell.

9¼ miles (14.8km), 4 hours. Easy, mostly downhill.

Here is an opportunity to ride on the little train to Jakobsbad again. Not only does the walk start by using this toylike transport, but all the effort of reaching the highest point of the walk is removed by using the Kronberg cable car. From that point the walking is almost all downhill.

This is a real lazy day walk, the sort which is more of a stroll than a walk, in which one spends all day over the expedition. Not only is the walk downhill, but evenly spaced gasthofs are waiting to provide tempting food.

The route holds the height gained from the cable car ride for a little while, before dropping fairly steeply to a pine-shrouded alp. The valley is simplicity itself; a gradually-improving track keeps well above the stream until at an easy crossing it changes sides, and this route is followed all the way down the main valley. Forest and farmland complete the way into Appenzell.

The Route

□ Reach Jakobsbad by train from Appenzell. Climb Kronberg — 5,458ft (1,663m), by its cable car. Restaurant facilities at the upper station.

The summit of Kronberg, a matter of only 100yd (91m) from the restaurant, is an ideal viewpoint for nearby Säntis – 8,215ft (2,350m), to the south. On a clear day the real giants of the Alps can be glimpsed further south and south-west, as a jumble of rock and snow.

□ Walk south across the scrub-covered col between Kronberg and its unnamed neighbour, towards the Dormees farmstead.

□ Take the left fork below the farm, then go down a steep grassy slope to a junction of five paths on the level alp below Schüzenälpli.

The area around Schüzenälpli is a good place for finding both alpine flowers and marmots.

□ Turn left, downhill, on a narrow spur between two mountain streams.

□ Leave the spur and enter the forest.

□ Follow the improving track of a forest road downhill for about 3¼ miles (5.2km), to Lehmen where there is a forest gasthof.

Appenzell

☐ Walk down the road, through forest away from Lehmen. At the far side of the forest turn left, away from the road on a track leading down to the River Wissbach.

Stones and other debris around the river crossing speak of the torrent which flows down the valley when the winter snows melt on the higher slopes.

☐ Cross the river and turn right to climb up to the group of farm buildings at Tüllen.

☐ Follow the north side of the valley on a steadily improving forest track.

☐ Turn left at Rechböhl to skirt the eastern edge of the Sonnenhalb forest. Then walk out on to the open, flat, main valley bottom.

☐ Cross a side road near Unterrain and follow the track opposite. Go through meadows and farmland into the southern outskirts of Appenzell.

AROSA

Map

Landeskarte der Schweiz (1:50,000 Series) Sheet 5002 — Arosa — Lenzerheide.

How to get there:

Road:

1 European motorways to Zürich, then south-east to Chur. Arosa is south-east at the head of the Schanfigger valley.
2 Black Forest and Lake Constance (Bodensee) to St Gallen. South to Feldkirch and Chur, then as above.

Rail:

Main line via Zürich and Chur, then branch lines to Arosa.

Air:

International airport at Zürich, then by train as above.

The Area

Famous ski resorts often suffer by being ignored during the period of the year when the snows are absent. This is a great pity, for the very factors which make them suitable as winter ski resorts, such as their setting, the angle of the nearby slopes and their share of sunshine, are all ideal qualifications for summer walking as well as winter skiing. Arosa is one such resort — famed for its winter facilities, but not so well known as an area suitable for summer walking.

Set on a sheltered alp high above the Schanfigger valley (the Schanfigger is a tributary of the Rhine), Arosa enjoys the maximum amount of sunshine. Walking is unlimited, either through forest, or on nearby meadows, or perhaps on the lower slopes of the Weisshorn and Hörnli. These summits are goals even for the average walker. Valleys radiating between the nearby peaks help to make Arosa a walker's paradise.

This once remote mountain village is almost traffic free. The road goes no further, and once the village is reached, there is little or no reason to use the car, unless it is for rare excursions into the lower valley; even then the excellent bus service or the railway should be used in preference to the effort of car driving.

Man has lived in this lovely area for many centuries. Throughout the Schanfigger valley, many of the buildings trace their origins to the thirteenth century, or even earlier.

The cable cars climbing to the top of both the Weisshorn and the Hörnli will give access to a land beyond compare. A day spent, for example, walking from one summit to the other, or perhaps using one of the downhill tracks back to Arosa, will rank high in the memory for years to come. With their knack of aniticipating mountain walkers' needs, conveniently-sited restaurants will satisfy appetites made keen by good healthy exercise.

There are many walks of a more ambitious nature which can be planned using Arosa as a base; walks such as the circuit of Schiesshorn combined with a visit to Alteinsee lake, or perhaps a visit to the Ramoz Hut in the upper valley, are possible excursions for the more energetic.

Arosa itself has much to offer as a break from mountain walking. There is nightlife with a friendly atmosphere, with most hotels taking turns in putting on some form of entertainment. Sheltered Lake Untersee has warmer water than one might expect at this altitude, and a swim in the late afternoon following a day in the mountains is a pleasant form of relaxation. Tennis courts can be found in the adjoining hamlets of Maran and Inner Arosa. Guided mountain walks of varying lengths, some visiting local Nature Reserves, are very much a feature of this area and should be considered by anyone who is uncertain of their ability to walk alone. The walks are also a convenient means of getting to know the area for the first-time visitor, and additionally, a way of meeting holidaymakers of other nationalities.

Useful Information

Tourist Office
Kurverein Arosa
CH 7500 Arosa
Telephone: 081 31 1621

Accommodation
Comfortable family-run hotels, some having five-star rating. Bed and breakfast apartments, youth hostels and one campsite.

Cable Cars
Hörnli   (gondola)
Weisshorn   (cabin)

Mountain Railway
Arosa is on a branch of the Rhaetian railway and connections can be made with places as far apart as Zermatt and St Moritz.

Golf
Nine hole course at Maran.

Alpine garden
Maran — 500yd (457m) east of tennis courts.

Rowing and Pedal Boats
Obersee Lake.

Trout Fishing
Obersee and Untersee.

Horse Riding
Weierhof — telephone: 081 31 1607

Tennis
Arosa and Maran

Swimming Pools
Covered   Altein Hotel
              Aparthotel Paradies
              Hotel Park
              Hotel Savoy
Open air   Untersee Lake
              Arosa Sports Hall

Indoor Ice Rink
Arosa Sports Hall

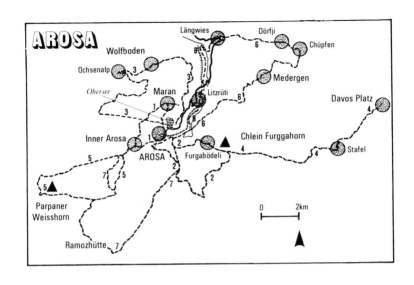

Inner Arosa

---

5 miles (8km), 2½ hours. Easy — 689ft (210m) ascent.

Arosa, with its elegant hotels, is spread along a sunny terrace of the Upper Schanfigg basin. Most of its buildings are modern, but the village is built on old foundations. The earliest building still standing is the fifteenth-century chapel built on a morainal mound above Old Arosa, showing that man has lived in this high sunny valley for many centuries.

The walk explores the town, taking in the Folk Museum on the way; with its fine record of the agricultural activities of the area, it also traces the development of Arosa as a popular winter sports resort.

The nearby hamlet of Maran is more isolated, and still retains much of the atmosphere of an alpine settlement. A visit to the nearby Alpine Garden completes the outward walk before the return to Arosa through shaded pine forest along the delightful Eichhornliweg (the 'squirrel path').

The Route

□ From the Verkersbüro (Information Centre), walk up the narrow street opposite and as far as the Catholic church.

□ Turn left along Sonnenbergstrasse. This quiet road climbs gradually above the town, skirting woodland, before joining the Poststrasse at Brüggli Platz near the bridge over the Melcherenbach stream.

□ Walk uphill past the Brüggli sports complex to Inner Arosa and the Heimat Museum.

The Heimat or Folk Museum is an interesting collection of local memorabilia in an old house built in the typical architectural style of the region; of special note is its overhanging roof, supported on massive beams and weighted with rocks to withstand both high wind and heavy snow.

□ Turn right behind the museum and follow the Kirchweg path up to the church.

Bergkirchli, or the Mountain Chapel, has stood here more or less in its present form since the latter part of the fifteenth century. Built on an elevated site on a moraine with a north/south axis, it is visible for a considerable distance throughout the upper valley. Thought to have been built originally by communal effort, some of the crude workmanship can still be seen and the chapel has been repaired many times. The interior is bare, but this tends to highlight its simplistic beauty; a tiny pedal organ with its intricate scrollwork is the only decoration.

□ Cross the valley by a rough path which aims directly towards the Tschuggenhütte restaurant. The ground may be boggy on either side of the stream, but rocky ground beyond it will be well drained and an easy, well made track leads up to the restaurant.

□ Follow a jeep track northwards, crossing a junction of tracks as far as the middle station of the Weisshorn cable car. There is a small restaurant here which would make an interesting lunch stop, during which one can watch the coming and going of cable cars.

□ Walk to the north-east, across open alpine meadows, downhill in the direction of Maran. Turn left on a well defined road, the Prätschliweg.

□ Follow the road into Maran (which is an alternative lunch stop).

□ Walk through the scattered villas and hotels of Maran towards the upper section of the golf course. Beyond it is the alpine garden.

The Alpengarten is a unique collection of alpine flowers found in the locality. They are shown off almost in their natural setting.

□ Walk back to Maran and turn left in front of the tennis courts.

□ Walk downhill on the gently sloping path of the Eichornliweg, through woodland with views below of the Obersee lake.

□ Enter Arosa above the railway station and join the main street close to the cinema and the information centre.

8 miles (12.8km), 5 hours (6 if climbing the Schiesshorn).
Moderate/strenuous — 2,599ft (792m) plus a further 637ft
(194m) to the summit of the Schiesshorn.

It is unfortunate, but at the beginning of this walk it is necessary to pass a cement factory and a sewage works. However, both are soon out of sight and mind and are a small price to pay for an interesting tour around this delightful little alpine peak.

The route crosses the Plessur valley away from Arosa, and climbs through deep pine forest along the Furggatobel valley into the realms of the high mountains. The summit of Schiesshorn can be taken, so to speak, in passing, before a rocky descent leads past the dramatic Alteiner waterfall.

A steep zigzag path reaches the broad Welschtobel valley where an easy track leads to Arosa.

The Route

□ From the main street walk down to the little square near the Evangelical church and turn left into Seewaldweg.

□ Follow this lane beyond Arosa and into forest, close by the south shore of the Untersee Lake.

□ Turn right and walk downhill, under the railway and past the cement factory.

□ Follow the narrow Iselweg road, which leads steeply downhill, across the middle of the ski jump and into the valley bottom.

□ Cross the Plessur river and walk past the sewage works.

□ Turn left beyond the sewage works and cross the flood plain of the Welschtobel river.

The width of the debris on this flat space speaks of the volume of water which flows each spring when the snows are melting.

□ Walk, in pine forest, around the top of land used by farmers of the Isel community.

□ Begin to climb through forest towards the mouth of the Furggatobel valley.

□ To gain height away from the narrowest part of the valley, the path, still in forest, swings away to the north (left); follow this to a footpath junction.

□ Turn right and climb into the open at the alp of Furggatobeli.

□ Walk across the alpine meadows and then through a sparse belt of pines towards the rocky slopes of the Chlein Furggahorn (*chlein* means little).

□ Climb steadily across the scree slopes to a path junction at the valley head.

□ Turn right to walk through the upper combe, as far as the broad col beneath the south-eastern slopes of the Schiesshorn.

The ascent of Schiesshorn – 8,550ft (2,605m) – is quite straight-forward. The path, which is signposted and waymarked, turns right at the col and aims directly at the summit, first across a grassy slope and finally on loose rock and turf. The view from the top takes in the Arosa valley and all the nearby peaks.

□ Walk downhill, away from the col, to a junction of paths above the tiny Alteinsee lake.

□ Turn right, downhill, on an increasingly steep and rocky path which follows the Alteinbach stream almost as far as the Alteiner waterfall.

It is necessary to make a short diversion, to the right, in order to see the waterfall which is highly recommended.

□ To avoid steep and potentially dangerous rocks, follow the path to the left and west away from the waterfall around a spur of the Leidflue ridge.

□ Walk down by the zigzag path through pine forest and alongside an open avalanche shoot (fortunately only a danger in late winter).

□ Join the valley path and turn right, downstream, along the Welschtobel river.

□ Turn left at the head of the flood plain and climb a little way through the Hinterwald pine forest, then around the shoulder of the hillside to cross the River Plessur at Müliboden.

□ Walk across the meadow and join the road at the side of the playing field. Turn right and walk uphill to Poststrasse and the main shopping streets of Arosa.

8½ miles (15.3km), 4-5 hours. Moderate.

The beauty of this walk is the fact that height gained easily by using the cable car to the summit of the Weisshorn — 8,707ft (2,653m) — is kept, carefully, for at least a third of the distance involved on this high-level route.

Basically, the walk follows the broad north-east ridge away from the summit of the Weisshorn, crossing or skirting a number of its satellites before swinging across the steeper northern spur and so down to remote Ochsenalp. The rest of the walk is spent following an easy track through a pine forest, which can, on a hot day, come as a welcome relief from the bare open hillside where shade is almost nonexistent. Breaks and clearings in the forest offer an ever-changing range of views of valley and peaks.

The Route

□ Take the two-stage cable car lift from behind the railway station to the top of the Weisshorn.

The view from the Weisshorn on a clear day ranges, in a clockwise direction, from the Silvretta group almost directly to the east, marking the Austro-Swiss border; Piz Bernina in the Diavolezza group above Pontresina is approximately south-south-east and on the Swiss-Italian border. Away in the distance, south-south-west, Monte Rosa can usually be seen with its famous neighbour, the Matterhorn, close by. The giants of the Bernese Oberland, grouped around the Jungfrau and Eiger, are a conglomerate mass of blues and white, west-south-west. North of the Weisshorn, the summits are not so spectacular, but Säntis can usually be found at north-north-west above the trench of the Rhine Valley.

□ Turn right and follow the ridge path away from the summit, downhill to the north-north-east across a broad scree-covered slope.

□ Walk down to a wide col and the Sattelhütte.

□ Keep left at the hut; go gradually downhill on grassy slopes with occasional small patches of scree, which can usually be avoided.

□ On reaching the top of a long line of broken cliffs, the path swings right to follow the narrowing ridge as far as the rocky combe head below Fuchs.

□ Downhill past a small pool to a footpath junction, west of Hauptichopf — 7,083ft (2,158m).

□ Go left over about half a mile (800m) of rocky broken ground to a footpath junction at the top of a small ridge.

□ Turn left to follow a well-made path over steadily improving high pasture. This is Ochsenalp, and from here the path gradually loses height as it rounds the end of the north ridge of the Brüggerhorn.

□ Go right on reaching the farmsteads at Ochsenalp, and leave the alpine meadows to enter the forest section of the walk.

At first the pines are scattered and stunted on this, the upper limits of the treeline, but later the shade is complete where the path enters more sheltered zones.

□ On reaching the clearing of the Wolfboden farmstead, keep left below the steep crags of Capätsch and walk past the farmhouse.

□ Re-enter the forest, keeping right at the junction with a forest track. Follow this to the east and then south around the shoulder of the Uf Prätsch hillside.

The shaded woodland often comes as a welcome relief, and occasional views add interest.

□ Ignoring side paths and forest tracks, follow the gently-descending track across the forested slope.

The ravine of Seebachtobel has been carved out by an ancient glacier, and later enlarged by floodwater overflowing; from the small lake, the Unter Prätschsee, at the top of a line of crags 1/4 mile (400m) to the west.

□ The track continues, descending almost all the way to the Obersee lake near Arosa.

4   DAVOS VIA THE MAIENFELDER PASS

---

11 miles (17.7km), 6 hours. Moderate/strenuous — 2,695ft (821m) ascent.

Walking from one mountain valley to another can be an exciting experience, because even today, with the advantages of easy travel, the isolation created by intervening ridges is still apparent. Cultures developed independently only six or seven miles apart, as shown by their differing architectural styles. Of course today's ubiquitous concrete hotels are the same everywhere, but an examination of the older buildings, the farmhouses and barns, reveals subtle differences between those around Arosa and Davos.

A linked town extending for 3 miles (4.8km), Davos developed early as a high-class winter sports resort; the slopes on either side of the broad, sunny Landwasser valley offer runs catering for every skier from absolute novices to olympic competitors. In winter, Davos boasts the largest outdoor skating rink in the world.

The walk crosses the Maienfelder Furgga (Pass), and then swings across the lower slopes of the Schwarzhorn before dropping into the Landwasser valley, entering Davos Platz conveniently near the railway station.

As the return journey by train is rather long, about 50 miles (80km), by way of Klosters, Landquart and Chur, check the train schedules beforehand, but allow plenty of time for the walk. Remember that once over the Maienfelder Pass the point of no return is soon passed.

The Route

□ Walk down to the Plessur river by way of the Untersee lake, the cement factory and sewage works. Hardly an auspicious start, but regretfully unavoidable without a wide detour.

□ Turn left beyond the boundary of the sewage works and cross the flood plain of the Welschtobel.

□ Follow the path, marked by white-red-white block symbols, around the wooded edge of the Isel meadows.

□ Climb through the pine forest, then across the rocky flood delta of the Furggatobel.

□ Follow the river for a little way upstream and move away, by path, uphill to the left; begin to climb the steep rocky slopes of the Chlein Furggahorn — 8,175ft (2,491m).

☐ Cross the open meadows of Furgabödeli and then through the thinning trees of the upper limits of the Furggawald forest.

☐ On rough ground, climb by a series of zigzags towards the more gentle slopes above.

☐ Keep straight on at the junction with the Schiesshorn path.

☐ Climb on a grassy path, between zones of scree and bare rock to the top of the Maienfelder Furgga — 8,008ft (2,440m).

☐ Ignore the climber's path to the left on the Arosa side of the pass.

The summit of the pass is marked by a tiny lake. Attractive views across the Plessur and Landwasser valleys.

☐ Begin to walk downhill; cross the complex of streams marking the headwaters of the Chummerbach river.

The path rounds a broad spur of the south-east ridge of the Schwarzhorn – 9,055ft (2,759m), itself a subsidiary of the slightly higher Tiejer Flue – 9,127ft (2,781m). As the path loses height it leaves the rocky alpine zone in favour of steadily improving pasture.

☐ Follow the path around the hillside to the group of farmsteads at Stafel.

A short cut is possible in case of tiredness or lack of time; at Stafel go right and downhill to the railway at Frauenkirch.

☐ Cross the wide combe of the Frauentobel and continue downhill on an improving track, now mostly within a mature pine forest, all the way to Davos Platz. The track enters the town at the side of the canalised Albertibach stream about 650yd (594m) from the railway station.

The countryside near Arosa

8 miles (12.8km), 5-6 hours. Moderate/strenuous — 2,908ft
(886m) descent after an initial high-level walk.

Here is another walk which starts from a high point, the height being gained effortlessly by the use of a cable way. In this case it is by the way of the gondola lift from Inner Arosa to the Hörnli col at 8,248ft (2,513m).

This height, as with the neighbouring Weisshorn walk, is held for a considerable portion of the walk before it is lost on the descent of the Plessur valley.

The high-level section of the walk is, in fact, the circuit of three sides of the Parpaner Weisshorn — 9,268ft (2,824m). The well-made path crosses rocky, often scree-covered slopes, but should be within the capabilities of anyone used to hill walking.

Hardier walkers may like to try the optional ascent of the Parpaner Rothorn, 9,390ft (2,861m), about one mile (1.6km) to the south of the Gredigs Fürggli (pass) at the beginning of the Plessur valley. If this option is taken, remember that it will take an extra two hours to cover the rocky ridge and regain the main route.

The Route

□ Take the bus along Poststrasse to the Kulm stop and walk along Hörnlistrasse to the bottom of the Hörnli gondola lift. Use the lift to reach the col. **NB:** the Hörnlihütte will be the only place offering refreshments on this walk.

□ Leave the upper station and restaurant by following the path over to the west side of the ridge.

□ Turn left, downhill, for a little way, across the grassy slope.

□ Ignoring a path to the right (to Urdensee) keep straight on, across the rocky slope and occasional patches of springy turf.

□ Turn left and climb to the narrow col, 8,399ft (2,550m), on the ridge below the Parpaner Weisshorn.

□ Go down the steep western slope, using the carefully designed zigzags of the path.

The rocky west face of the Parpaner Weisshorn, being well drained and open to the sun, encourages the growth of small cushion alpine plants like the saxifrages and moss campion; the deep blue of gentians will also be seen, lower down the mountain.

☐ Climb steadily across scree slopes and around the mountain shoulder to the narrow rocky defile of the Gredigs Fürggli pass — 8,589ft (2,617m).

The pass offers shade on a hot day for anyone waiting while others climb the Parpaner Rothorn. The route to the latter is waymarked with the usual white-red-white block symbols. First skirting the steep crags immediately to the south of the col, it then follows the east side of the knobbly ridge in a more or less direct line to the summit. Return by the same route.

Do not attempt to follow the route beyond the top of the Parpaner Rothorn, as it involves some tricky rock climbing.

☐ Walk down to the scree-coverd upper combe of the Plessur, beneath the south wall of the Parpaner Weisshorn.

☐ Follow the path downhill and on to gentler, grass-covered slopes above the Plessur stream.

☐ Pass a remote farm and the north side of the Alplisee lake.

☐ Beyond the lake the path drops suddenly over the steep Chlus crag. Take care and use the zigzag path.

Chlus marks the lip of the upper or hanging valley, a feature of this one time glacial zone.

☐ Turn right at a junction on the upper edge of pasture belonging to a series of small farms.

☐ Cross the stream and turn left at the next path junction. Walk steeply downhill on the grassy path beneath a prominent crag.

☐ Walk by the side of the Schwellisee lake, and cross its outflow at the wooden bridge.

The Schwellisee will make an ideal rest stop almost at the end of the walk.

☐ Follow the path into Inner Arosa and either catch the bus back or walk the rest of the way along the main street.

---

10 miles (16km), 5 hours. Moderate — 1,569ft (478m) ascent.

To the east of the Plessur valley and above the treeline there is an area of comparatively flat land. Sheltered from the east by a wall of rocky peaks marking the division between Davos and Arosa, the land has been used by generations of farmers. Taking advantage of its sheltered sunny position, they take their cattle and sheep to these high pastures as soon as the grass has grown sufficiently, after winter snows, to allow the animals to graze. Milk is made into cheese and butter which is carried down from time to time to valley co-operatives.

The walk visits four of these settlements where the walker, a rare visitor in these parts, is sure of a friendly welcome. Anyone who takes the trouble of coping with the rather difficult dialect will be rewarded by conversations with interesting people, full of character. One or two farms are likely to have beer or milk and perhaps a slice or two of dry smoked ham for sale.

Check train times from Längwies to Arosa before setting out.

The Route

□ Walk out of Arosa along Seewaldweg, past the Untersee lake and down through forest into the valley alongside the railway line.

□ Fork right at the signposted path, over the railway and down to the Stausee lake.

□ Follow the narrow northern neck of the lake, across the outflowing river as far as a path to the left.

□ Turn left from the lake, climbing easily out of the forest and over the Furggenalp.

□ Cross a small stream and enter mature pine forest.

□ Climb through the Tiejer Wald forest, steeply at times, around the shoulder of Tiejer Hauptji.

□ Leave the forest and walk through a boulderfield then down to the river.

□ Cross the river, the Tiejer Bach, and climb to a footpath junction.

□ Turn left, on more level ground now and walk past the farmsteads of Tieja and Tschuggen.

☐ Walk across the delightful alpine pasture, swinging round the shoulder of the hill as the footpath turns north-east.

☐ Ignore a path on the left, cross two small streams and reach Medergen.

Medergen, like the three other summer settlements visited on this walk, is an interesting conglomeration of timber houses and barns which have probably stood here for decades. Some are lifted above ground level on a series of mushroom-like combinations of stones designed to stop rats climbing into the storage space above.

☐ Turn right away from the centre of Medergen and walk towards, and then round a prominent grassy ridge barring the way to the east.

☐ To the north of the ridge, Wangegg, where the ground is a little stonier, walk past a small pool then go steeply down into the Chüpfer Talli valley.

☐ Cross the stream and turn left to follow it downstream, until the path bears right away from the stream towards the main valley of the Hauptertällibach.

☐ Cross the river and climb up to Chüpfen 'village'.

☐ Turn left at Chüpfen and walk downhill on a steadily improving path through the settlements of Schmitten and Dörfji.

☐ Three tracks leave Dörfji; take the lower, to the left into a narrower section of this high valley.

☐ The path, which by now is a jeep track, runs downhill in a series of bends towards the forested lower slopes.

☐ Turn left at a junction in the valley bottom and then right on reaching the main road.

☐ Follow the road to Längwies village and turn left in the central square.

☐ Walk down to the railway station to catch the train back to Arosa.

7 ERZHORNSATTEL FROM THE RAMOZHÜTTE

12½ miles (20km), 7-8 hours. Strenuous — 4,923ft (1,125m) ascent.

Anyone familiar with the upper Plessur valley (walk 5) will be conscious of the steep wall of rocky peaks on its south side. Looking from the vantage point on easier ground above the Alplisee lake, to the stream draining the northern combe of the Aroser Rothorn, they may have noted a narrow gap in the ridge to the east of the peak, before it rises to the next summit, the Erzhorn. This gap, the Erzhornsattel — 9,006ft (2,744m), is the crux of the walk.

To reach the pass is no mean feat; the walk is tough and the path often difficult, but having completed this high-level excursion, it will remain in the memory for many years.

The route is simple enough; it follows the Welschtobel valley almost to its source, calling at the Swiss Alpine Club's Ramoz hut on the way. Steep climbing is necessary to reach the pass, with a hard downhill section into the Plessur valley.

As there is a considerable amount of rock to cross on both sides of the Erzhornsattel, boots are essential footwear on this walk.

The Route

□ Walk along the Seewaldweg to the cement factory and follow the roadway under the railway and down to the sewage works.

□ Walk upstream along the edge of the pine forest and flood plain of the Welschtobelbach river.

□ Ignore side paths and follow the main path, steadily uphill, through the forest.

The initial forested part of this walk is easy and a steady pace should be maintained for most of the way.

□ Leave the forest for the rocky middle valley. Cross the river at the wooden bridge and turn right upstream.

□ Walk on sparse turf and rocky ground, climbing all the while and following the white-red-white waymarks.

There is a narrow ravine which marks the beginning of the upper valley. The path divides and it does not matter which one is used, although the lefthand path faces away from the sun, and therefore the view will be clearer.

☐ Turn right above the ravine, cross the river to reach Ramozhütte.

The hut will be welcome but try not to stay too long as it is only at the start of the hardest part of the walk.

☐ Climb away from the hut, initially on steep rocky ground, which eases for a little way across a grassy alp.

Above the alp the way is sometimes unclear, but by looking for and following the waymarks you should not go wrong.

☐ Climb steeply up a scree-filled rocky combe, to the pass of the Erzhornsattel.

There is evidence of mining in the Arosa area and the word Erzhorn (Erz is 'ore') possibly has some connection with metallic staining of the nearby rocks.

☐ The way down from the pass is steep and over rocky ground. Take great care and do not rush things. Follow the waymarked route, zigzagging across rocky outcrops and the lower scree slopes.

☐ Follow the path away from the scree around the foot of the outlying crags into the green alpine pastures of the Plessur valley.

☐ Turn right on the valley path downhill past the Alplisee lake to the rock outcrops of Chlus.

☐ Take the left fork below Chlus and follow this path through the upper pastures of Inner Arosa.

The Mountain Chapel at Inner Arosa (see Walk 1)

A VALLEY WALK

5½ miles (9km), 2-3 hours. Easy.

The final walk in the Arosa itinerary is included as a suggestion for something to do when rain prevents more ambitious expeditions further afield. With luck, the weather will remain fine and sunny for the whole holiday in Arosa, and a walk to fill in the time between showers may not be needed. Having said that, however, the walk should not be ignored in the event of fine weather. Most of the way, it is beneath the shade of tall pine trees and is also suitable for days when the sun is too hot for comfortable walking.

The route is simple; it follows the valley with the river never far away, and has the small village of Litzirüti conveniently stationed halfway. Längwies has a fine selection of small gasthofs and cafés and marks the finish of the walk. The train is used to return to base.

Tracks and footpaths which climb away from the central section of the route can be used to extend the walk if needed.

The Route

☐ Walk by way of Untersee down to the cement works road.

☐ Cross the road and walk along Ausserwaldweg, at the side of the railway.

☐ Ignore paths to the left and right of the railway, go over swampy Ronggried, to recross the track.

☐ Walk parallel to the railway, as far as the valley road. Turn right and follow the road, downhill, as far as the works access road.

☐ Turn right and walk past the Brünst factory.

☐ Go through a short stretch of forest and out into a clearing in front of Litzirüti village.

☐ Take the road opposite the station approach and away from the main road.

☐ Walk out of the village on a forest access road, roughly parallel to the railway.

☐ Where both road and railway enter the forest, turn right over the latter, at first across an open meadow then along the forest edge. Finally enter the forest beyond a group of barns.

☐ The narrow path threads its unmarked way through the forest. At first it keeps well back from the river, but soon follows the western (left) bank.

Solitude broken only by the occasional whistle of a passing train completes this riverside walk. Bird and plant life are plentiful, especially near the river.

□ Join a cross-valley track at a junction with a third path.

□ Turn sharp right to follow the track downhill, then over the river.

□ Climb between landslips, still in forest, across a tiny side valley, the Sapüner Bach.

□ Climb the opposite side of the valley, leaving the forest for fields surrounding the village of Längwies.

The railway station is to the left and the main village with its shops, gasthofs and restaurants is to the right at the top of a small slope.

The Untersee at Arosa